An American Life

To Jim

I am happy to sign this
book for a nice
friend,

Best Wishes
Jimmy Gentry

AN AMERICAN LIFE

JIMMY GENTRY

EDITED BY PAUL CLEMENTS
ILLUSTRATIONS BY JIMMY GENTRY
COORDINATED BY GALE PAYNE

THIS BOOK WAS MADE POSSIBLE THROUGH
THE GENEROSITY OF
WILLIAM AND JENNIFER FRIST

FIRST EDITION

ISBN 0-9724078-0-4

Library of Congress Control Number: 2002111947

Cover Design by Emily Bowman

Pleasantview Press
1970 Hwy. 96 West
Franklin, TN 37064

To my mother,
my wife Rebecca,
and
my brother David

CONTENTS

PROLOGUE

In 1945, as a soldier in the Army of Occupation, I was one of four Americans who were temporarily stationed in the mountain village of Feldkirchen, Austria, on the Swiss border. It was one of the most beautiful places in the world, and forty-two years later I went back to Feldkirchen with my wife, Rebecca.

It was not the way I remembered it. The mountain stream that had flowed through the village had been covered over with pavement, and modern buildings had been built above the stream. The picturesque little bridges that had connected the two sides of the village were, of course, gone too. Feldkirchen was just another town.

FELDKIRCHEN, AUSTRIA 1945

We checked into a motel that had been built after the war. Rebecca set out to shop while I went to find out what happened to the beautiful little mountainside village. I walked down to the corner where a group of people were waiting at an intersection to cross over to my side of the street. The light changed and as they came toward me I picked out the oldest man I saw, and I asked him, "Do you speak English?" He looked at me and said, "Where are you from?" He had just a trace of an accent. I was startled by his command of English and by his question, "Where are you from?" I started to say Nash-ville, Tennessee, because he may have been able to connect country music to Nashville, but instead I answered, "Franklin, Tennessee." The man repeated "Franklin, Tennessee—the best place in the world." I couldn't believe what he'd said. "Sir? How do you know anything about Franklin, Tennessee?" He went on to tell me that he had been an Austrian in the German Army, fighting in North Africa. When he was captured he had been sent to Camp Campbell, Kentucky, as a prisoner of war.

"Each morning at Camp Campbell we were loaded on trucks and sent to towns around Kentucky and Tennessee to help with farm work. I was one of a group that came to Franklin each morning. We assembled at the corner of Third Avenue and the town square, beside the courthouse next to Mrs. Smithwick's pie wagon. I wanted to stay in Franklin after the war, but they wouldn't let me, so I had to leave. I wish I was there now. Will you take me back to Franklin with you?"

We couldn't take him back to Franklin, but I understood why he wanted to go. There is a lot I want to say about the place I grew up, and how it changed after the war, so I need to go back to the beginning...

BEGINNINGS

Chapter One

"In the beginning God..." The first four words in the Bible were used on the first day of each school year by Mr. Daly Thompson, the beloved principal of Franklin High School. "In the beginning God..." Those words will always be true.

Today I can think of no better way to start telling about my life than to say, before anything else, in the beginning God allowed me to be born into a large family with a loving mother and father. But what I know about the history of my family starts a long time before I was born.

Three Gentry brothers from North Carolina came over the mountains back in the late 1700s or early 1800s, and the tradition in our family is that two of them were scalped by the Indians, and the one who escaped went back to North Carolina. That is my earliest knowledge of my father's family.

My daddy, Zebulon B. Gentry, was born in 1875 near Marshall, in the mountains of North Carolina, where he was raised along with six brothers and sisters. He served in the Spanish-American War and went on to get a job with the Bell Telephone Company. He was involved in building phone lines from Birmingham to Nashville, and when he was working south of Franklin in Maury County, he met my mother. Her name was Gertrude Butner. She was born in Coffee County in 1887, and grew up in Maury County, just south of Spring Hill near a little place called Neapolis. When the telephone lines were coming through, my mother got a job cooking for the workers and she met my father. Her father, John Butner, objected to the marriage at first, and my father left to work down in Florida for awhile. It wasn't too long before he came back, and he and my mother were married in 1906.

They lived in Asheville, North Carolina, where my two eldest sisters were born—Jesse in 1907 and Louise in 1911. Then, with my father still working for Bell Telephone, they moved to Cullman, Alabama, which only had six or eight telephones. My mother operated the switchboard during the day and my daddy operated it at night. My daddy worked two jobs. While they were in Cullman, he picked cotton. He was paid by weight, and the man in charge of the scales was short-changing the workers. My daddy got into a fight with him and ended up hitting the man in the head with one of the weights. The sheriff came, but my daddy didn't get arrested.

Daddy and Mama in 1906.

Later on they moved to Birmingham where my sister Dorthy was born in 1914, and they moved from there to Williamson County. They lived in various rental houses in and around Franklin, and the family kept on growing. After having three girls, Mama started having boys. My brother William was born in 1916, and my brother Dan came along in 1919.

When my brother David was born in 1922, our family was living in the Cannon house on Nashville Pike, about a mile north of Franklin. My oldest sister, Jesse Lee, had married and moved into the house with her husband, Horace Harmon. He died of lung disease a little before the birth of their daughter, Frances. She was three months older than I was, and although she was actually my niece, we would be raised together, and I didn't learn until many years later that Frances wasn't my sister.

We were still living in the Cannon house, which would later become known as Wyatt Hall, when I was born there on November 28,
1925, with the help of Dr. Toon Nolen. Before I was two years old, we moved to a house on West Main Street in Franklin, where my

brother, Bobby, was born in 1927. My earliest memories are from when I was three or four years old and living in that house in Franklin. West Main was a gravel road, and

an automobile wouldn't come by more than about once an hour. Almost as many horse-drawn wagons as cars came down West Main, and I was more interested in the wagons because of the horses. There is something about a living creature that gets the attention of small children.

Across the road was the office of a little oil company operated by Mr. Bill Cameron and Mr. Fleming Williams. Two doors down from us was Mr. Wright's coal yard. I remember things like my mother putting me down for a nap, and then I would get up and peek out of the window so I could watch my brother going down to a nearby creek to play. I remember Mama's brother, Uncle George Butner, coming to visit. He would sit out in the front and whittle. He had white hair and a white moustache, and I liked to hear him talk. We had a little dog named Tricksy, and when Uncle George would see children coming back from the coal yard pulling a wagon load of coal, he would sick Tricksy on them. He got a kick out of seeing them run and maybe turning over their wagon.

I always had plenty of playmates at our house, whether it was my brothers or puppies or baby chicks. God created the heavens and earth, and then he turned his

Me, Frances, and Bobby in front, Dan and David in the back.

attention to creating flying, crawling, and creeping creatures. He must have had little children in mind when he created puppies and baby chicks. There is nothing like holding a little soft, fuzzy chick cupped in your hands and studying those little round black eyes set in soft yellow fuzz. Lessons of life are learned from nature, and those lessons can carry over into the rest of our lives. There's some-

thing wonderful about watching a baby chick scurry under the protective wings of the mama hen.

Me with my leg braces and a rooster.

Playing with chicks and puppies became a little harder for me at an early age, because I had to wear steel braces on both of my legs. A shortage of vitamin D had led to a disease called rickets, and that had caused my legs to bow. One time I got into trouble because I liked to climb. I was climbing on Mr. Riley Lawson's chicken house roost, and when I fell I caught one of my braces on a nail. I stayed there for a pretty good while before Aunt Hattie Mitchell, the black lady who helped my mother, found me hanging upside down.

We thought of Aunt Hattie as a part of our family. She helped my mother with housework and cleaning and washing. I remember Aunt Hattie loading our coaster wagon with dirty clothes and bed linens, and putting me up on top of the pile for a ride up West Main to Eleventh Avenue. We would turn right by Mr. Alley's

13

and go to Aunt Hattie's house, which was just off Eleventh Avenue. She would do her wash in a big black kettle in her backyard, and she would sing while she worked. She would let me get just close enough to the fire so I could throw in a stick now and then. James Mitchell, her husband, and her son Pap would come home for lunch, and I would eat with them before she took me back home.

I had a good relationship with the black people I knew. I still run into people who ask me where I am from. I'll say I'm from Tennessee, and they say I must be from somewhere farther south. The reason might be because I got some of my language and dialect from the black people I grew up around.

I remember starting to school when I was six years old. I knew something was changing when Mama dressed me in my good clothes and lick-parted my hair. She took me by the hand and we walked up the sidewalk along West Main, by Mr. Alley's, by Miss Susie Gentry's, then on by Dr. Nolen's, the Brittain's, and Miss Sallie Seay's. Four blocks later we got to the intersection where Main Street and Fifth Avenue and Columbia Avenue all come together, known as Five Points. There, on a triangle-shaped lot right beside the Cumberland Presbyterian Church, was Franklin Elementary School.

Franklin Elementary School

Mama left me with a teacher, and then we were herded upstairs to an auditorium where there was an old man with white hair named Mr. A. J. Haun. He looked to be at least 100 years old. Mr. Haun talked for a little while and I didn't really understand anything he said. We all got up and went downstairs, so I thought it was time to leave. I thought, "There's nothing to going to school," and I headed home. Four blocks later I was home, but then Mama saw me and four blocks later I was back at school again.

During the first years of elementary school we had small rugs, which we used for our daily naps. Every day before our nap we had a prayer. One time Miss Helen Jordan, our second grade teacher, asked the class to bow our heads and close our eyes. About halfway through the prayer a boy named Glen said, "Miss Helen, Gail's eyes aren't closed." Miss Helen simply remarked, "How do you know?" There was a good lesson there. Those who find fault with others are likely to have faults of their own.

During recess, the area on one side of the school, along Columbia Avenue, was for boys, and the other side, along West Main, was for the girls. The girls' side had a couple of shade trees; the boys' side had no shade. If a ball rolled over on the girls' side, no boy would dare go get it. Sometimes somebody would try to push somebody else over to the girls' side. We didn't want anybody to see us over there with those girls. On the boys' side we had a real cannon that had been given to the town of Franklin. The cannon was important to us because we could use tablet paper and draw up hundreds and hundreds of dollars, and then hide the money in the barrel of the cannon. Then we would protect it from the gangs who were trying to get to the cannon and rob the bank.

Moon Mullins, the school janitor, would tend to the coal furnace, and he would empty the cinders on the playground, which was bare of grass. We got plenty of cuts and scrapes when we fell down. There would be lots of running, yelling, and chasing until Mr. Haun blew his brass horn signaling the end of recess.

LIFE ON LEWISBURG PIKE

Chapter Two

From West Main we moved to 145 Lewisburg Pike, to the old Rolff house. Mr. Tom McCall lived next door, Mr. Frank North lived across the street, and Captain Tom Henderson, a famous World War I veteran, lived a little farther out Lewisburg Pike. The railroad tracks  ran right behind our house, and just across the tracks was a black community. My best friend from over there was Tigg Poynter. We were about the same age. We went fishing once or twice—the Harpeth River was right down the hill—but we usually just played around the neighborhood.

One day Tigg was sitting on a fence post, and I picked up a clod of dirt and threw it at him. I was just playing around, but I hit him in the head. He fell off the post and went home crying, and when his mother told my mother, I got a whipping. Mama was the disciplinarian at our house most of the time. She would take a switch to us, and a switch hurt on our bare legs more than anything. We'd promise never to do whatever we'd done ever again, if she would just stop.

Sometimes things got pretty lively around our house. One day my brother Dan went fishing with a group of black boys. One of them was named German Meeks. They were always fishing together. On this particular day they were fishing illegally. They were using a seine, which is a large fishing net, and seines were illegal. They caught a sack full of fish, and I think Dan, who was younger than the rest of them, was carrying the sack. So a police car showed up, and the boys all took off running through the bushes and trees.

I was playing in the yard, and all of a sudden Dan came rushing up from the river. He was all wet, and just running as hard as he could. He ran in and slammed the back door. I didn't know what was going on. In a little while Mr. Oscar Garner, one of the two or three policemen in Franklin, came up. He asked me if Dan was there, and I said, "Yes sir, he is." He said to tell Dan to come out. In a little while Dan came out just as clean and neat as he could be. He said to Dan, "I don't know if you were down there with those other guys or not." I think he suspected him, and he should have known something was going on—Dan didn't ever stay that clean.

We did a lot of playing around the railroad track. Sometimes we would put down a penny on the rail and the train would run over it and flatten it out good. We couldn't go any higher than a penny though—no nickels and dimes—that was too expensive. Tigg and his friends would go way up the track south of Franklin and jump on the train when it began to slow down. The trains had coal cars, so as the boys rode in toward town, they would throw off coal all along the way, and when they got to Franklin, they would jump off. An hour or two later they would go back with a coaster wagon and pick up all the coal they'd dropped off and take it home. Sometimes there would be a train going real slow, and we didn't want to wait for it to finally go on by. We would roll underneath and then roll

17

out on the other side before the back wheels got there. We didn't think about what would've happened if we'd hit our heads or something. It was a stupid thing to do, but nobody ever got hurt.

Living so close to the railroad tracks during the Depression, we saw a lot of hobos. They came to our house all the time, and I was afraid of them. I would peep out the window and watch them. They would come and knock on the door and ask for food, and my mother would say, "All right, I will get you something to eat if you go over there and split that wood for me." I didn't see anything bad about them, but I was still afraid. It seemed like we were getting more and more hobos, and then we found that they had tied a white cloth on a tree down by the track. It was a signal, which meant here is a house where you can get food. When mama found out about the cloth, she said, "Go take that thing down."

My father's brother, Uncle Henry Gentry, was a hobo but I didn't look at him that way. He got off the train at the end of Third Avenue one day and walked down to our house. He came to spend the weekend and stayed a few years. He drank, but my daddy didn't allow any whiskey in the house. My daddy said, "Henry, you can stay as long as you want, but if you ever get drunk, leave and don't come back." There was also Aunt Emma, my daddy's unmarried sister. She stayed with us a lot over the years, and helped Mama with the cooking and cleaning up, but Aunt Donna Gunter, Mama's sister, was our favorite. Every time she came she would bring us a bag of candy.

Along with my uncle and two aunts, I got to know Mr. Sam

Johnson, a friend of my family's who lived down in Maury County between Neapolis and Columbia. He had a big farm back in the hills, and I loved going to visit Mr. Sam. We would play in his barn, and in the fall, when it got cold, he would kill hogs. Killing hogs and selling hams and sausage and meat was what he did for a living. Hog killings always took place in cold weather so the body of the hog would cool down fast. That kept the meat from spoiling.

He would get the hogs in a pen and shoot them in the head. Then he would hang the hogs up from a gambrel stick that he ran through their back legs. The pole was six or seven feet off the ground, and Mr. Sam would split open the hog's belly and remove the heart, lungs, liver, and all the other organs. The intestines were called chitlins, and they were taken to the creek and washed inside and out. After being gutted, the hog was lowered into a vat of scalding water so the hair could be scraped off.

Then the hog was hung back up, and the hair was removed. I watched Mr. Sam do the butchering. The back legs were called hams, and the front legs were shoulders. The flanks became bacon, and he also cut chops and backstrips. The scraps were used to make sausage. The meat would be put in a big wooden box filled with salt, which removed moisture from the meat. He would hang the meat in a smokehouse over a hickory fire, which gave it extra flavor. When the meat was preserved that way, it would be good for several years.

One time I went to Mr. Sam's in the summertime. I used to love running around in his yard with his dogs. He had five or six swarms of bees in his side yard, and I kept watching those bees going in and out of the hives. So I found a long pole, and I decided that I would put that stick in the hole and rattle it around a little

and see what was going on in there. Well, I found out. The dogs got stung, I got stung, and I had to run for my life. I learned not to mess around with bees when they were working.

Another person I especially remember was Harry Guffee, who was our iceman. He was delivering ice as a part-time job while he

was in school at Vanderbilt. Harry would deliver the ice using a horse and wagon. The amount to be left at each house was determined by an ice card hanging on the porch—25, 50, 75, or 100 pounds. We really liked Harry Guffee. On hot days he would take his ice pick and chip off little pieces of ice and give them to us. And I remember Uncle Harry Marsh, an old black gentleman who had a horse and carriage,

which was the only horse-drawn taxi in Franklin. When he would pick up the ladies on cold days, he would spread a buggy blanket over their laps and drive them to town so they could do their shopping.

All of the children in our family had chores to do. The girls helped with cleaning the house and things like that. The older boys would split the wood, and Bobby and I would bring in the kindling or carry buckets to the barn for our daddy. I loved to do work for my daddy. Mama would pour warm water into the bucket and I would take it out to the barn. Then my father would use a cloth flour sack to wash off the bag of our old milk cow. The bucket would be about a third full of water, and he would take that bucket and swing it over the top of his head. I couldn't figure out why that water didn't come out of the bucket. I thought it was magic.

Mama always kept empty 100-pound flour and sugar sacks at our house. They were used for wash cloths, tea towels, and for straining fresh milk from the barn. She would also use the bags to make shirts for the younger children. Mama would say that some people didn't have any shirts at all. She said that we might not have the best clothes, but we would always have the cleanest.

I've heard people talk about walking to school, and it sounds like an ordeal, but it was not that way for me. I usually got to walk with my friends, but sometimes I went by  myself. All the sidewalks led downtown when we were living on Lewisburg Pike in the Rolff House. Downtown Franklin—Main Street—was four blocks away. There wasn't a sidewalk in front of our house, so we would walk in the street until we reached the one at the fork of Adams Street and Lewisburg Pike. The concrete sidewalks were put down by John Scruggs, a skillful black man who imprinted his name in the wet concrete. His name became well known to everybody who used the sidewalks in Franklin.

We would walk along Adams Street under the maples and oaks and past the Jefferson's yard. They had a beautiful yellowwood tree, and in the spring I loved to look at its drooping white flowers. Farther on, the sidewalk went on either side of two large trees that were left standing in its path. Skaters liked to veer around them without slowing down. Beyond Margin Street, Adams Street was called by a different name—Fifth Avenue, and soon we would come to the rock wall that stood on two sides of the First Presbyterian Church. The more daring kids would climb up and walk on top of that wall, and go on around the angle it made at the corner of Main Street.

The wall was right at Five Points, and Franklin Elementary was just across the street. I can remember the school sidewalk leading straight up to the front door. Of course, if we weren't doing chores or going to school, we were usually playing, and if we weren't down at the river or on the train track or out in the yard, there was a good chance we were climbing trees.

Climbing trees was a specialty for a lot of boys back then. We wanted to climb every tree in the woods, and we knew how to climb them. People would say, "How are you going to climb that big old tree?" Well, we would pull a limb down and then go up that limb to the trunk and then climb up from there. You couldn't just shimmy up a big tree. We loved to climb trees. Every tree was a challenge. If a tree was there it was supposed to be climbed. Trees were so important to us. I believe that God put those trees here for the fruit and the timber, and for the birds and the beauty and the shade, but I think he also had in mind, "I am going to put these trees here for boys to climb."

I climbed just about every tree in our neighborhood and I got to be an expert, but I had a few falls along the way. Aunt Hattie was still with us after we moved out onto Lewisburg Pike, and one day I fell out of a tree and landed on my back. It knocked all the wind out of me. Aunt Hattie scooped me up and pounded my back until I could breathe again. She said, "Boy, you are going to kill yourself if you don't stop climbing in those trees."

Aunt Hattie Mitchell died while we were living on Lewisburg Pike. My sister Dorthy went to Aunt Hattie's house and found that

her body had been clothed in an old dress that had belonged to Mama's sister, Aunt Donna. James, Aunt Hattie's husband said, "That was all she had." So Dorthy went to town and bought a new dress for Aunt Hattie to have on, and she put a nice pin on the dress.

Aunt Hattie holding a neighbor's child with me, David, Dan, and Francis.

I was around black people the whole time I was growing up. I grew up with them, but I knew I didn't go to school with them, and I knew they didn't go to our church. I had great respect for a lot of the black people I knew, but it seemed like they were supposed to go one place and I was supposed to go somewhere else. We were together a lot as children, but over a period of time we segregated ourselves. That's just the way it was, but that didn't make it right.

DADDY AND THE COUNTRY

Chapter Three

Around 1935, when I was in about the fourth grade, we left Lewisburg Pike and moved across the Harpeth River to a farmhouse out on Murfreesboro Pike—about a mile and a half to the northeast. Moving to the country was one of the best things that ever happened to me. I was so proud to  live out there. I had reached an age where I could get out on my own and explore, and we had fields and creeks and woods all around us.

My daddy did not have any formal education, and neither did my mother. They grew up during a time when education was not a priority. Survival was the priority up in the hills around Marshall, North Carolina, and down on the farm near Neapolis, in Maury

County. My daddy worked hard to support our family. His days started around 5 a.m. with a trip to the barn to milk the cows. We liked to go with him to milk. We'd watch him wash off the bag and the teats of our two cows, and sometimes he would squirt us with milk while we tried to dart by without getting hit. After milking he would let us carry the bucket back to the house, where my mother strained and cooled the milk.

At breakfast Mama would usually fix eggs, grits, bacon, sausage, and biscuits stacked so high you might not be able to see who was sitting across the table. The only thing that had been bought in a store was the flour she used, and maybe some baking powder. And she always had her homemade jams and jellies on the table. Around the table would be my mother, my father, and the six children who were still at home—my brother, William, had married and moved away—and whichever aunt or uncle happened to be living with us at the time. We learned to share pretty early. If one of us was still hungry and somebody else had something left on the plate, the hungry one would say, "Are you going to eat that? Let me borrow it and I'll pay you back tomorrow." Maybe they'd get a slice of bacon, and the next morning a piece of bacon would go back the other way. After we ate, Daddy would give us instructions as to what needed to be done while he was at work.

Daddy still worked for Bell Telephone. He and Mr. L. L. Fiveash took care of all the lines in Williamson County, and Lillian Wauford or Mrs. Bessie Ormes ran the switchboard, while Mr. J. A. Harding ran the office. That was the whole company. My daddy would set the poles all by himself. He would use a post hole digger to dig the hole, and then he would put up the pole and string the wire.

One of the highlights of my life was going to work with my daddy. We didn't have an automobile, so the ride in the company truck was something special, and there was just the delight I took in being with my daddy. I hoped the trips would last a long time.

25

Sometimes he took me several miles out in the country. While he dug holes, or climbed poles with his spurs, it gave me time to explore and investigate new territory. When lunchtime came, it was customary for the lady of the nearest house to invite whoever was out working in to eat.

I remember riding out with him to Triune one day. I was throwing rocks and playing in the ditch while he was up on a pole, and when lunchtime came Mrs. Redmond came out of her house and said, "Mr. Gentry, you and your boy come on in, dinner is ready." We went in and she had fixed the nicest meal. I had already been in her barn looking around, and I found some little pigeon squabs, and I loved anything like that. I had told Daddy about them, and he said, "My boy said you had some squabs. Do you mind if we get them?" Mrs. Redmond said she didn't want them. Boy, that tickled me to death, so as soon as I got through eating, I went out there and got those squabs and took them home.

My daddy knew that we liked little creatures, so in his travels over the county he would run across things like little bantam chicks, and one time he brought home a lamb that had lost its mother. We got a big bottle with a nipple and raised that lamb to a full-grown sheep.

Mr. John Campbell lived across the road from us, and he raised sheep. Every once in a while something would happen and he'd have orphan lambs. He would give them to us, and we would have a lot of fun raising those lambs. If they got out in the pasture and a flood came along, their wool would get heavy. Since lambs can't swim, we would have to rush down and drag them out of the water. We would raise them up and my daddy would sell them. If we got four or five dollars, we thought we were really rich. Mr. Campbell was a good neighbor. He ran a mule barn in Franklin, and in the early spring, when Daddy was getting ready for planting, he'd borrow one of Mr. Campbell's mules and prepare our garden.

Sometimes Daddy would take us down to the river to fish or go swimming, but the older we got, the more interested we were in athletics. There was a little flat area down in front of our house where we would play baseball and football. Daddy didn't have any background in athletics, but he would try to play with us. We used to get tickled at him  because he didn't know what he was doing. He wasn't good at sports, but he didn't have to be good. Just playing with us was enough. My oldest brother, William, had a big part in my love of sports. He loved Vanderbilt, and he loved the New York Yankees. When I was learning to play baseball, he taught me to bat left handed, and I hit from the left side my whole life.

We loved our daddy, and we had great respect for him because he would be tough on us when he needed to be. One time Daddy opened two or three furrows with a plow and mule, and he

asked us to plant corn in there. He was planning to cover the corn we'd planted when he got home in the afternoon. We got to the end of one row, and then we decided we needed to go hear the new radio Mr. Robert Sewell had gotten. We had never heard a radio before. So we put all the corn in a hole and covered it with a rock and went over to the Sewell's. When Daddy got home, he found that there

was no corn in the furrows and we got a good whipping.

We had an apple orchard, and one day he asked us to pick apples. He told us to stay out of the creek. He knew if we got in the creek that we wouldn't get any work done.

After a while we figured we could justify going to the creek by saying the apples needed washing. We took them down there, washed them, and then we forgot all about them. The apples floated down to a little dam we had built, and our hogs waded out there and ate the apples. We got a good whipping that time too.

He would say, "Boys, when I get through with you, your hides won't hold shucks." We knew exactly what that meant. Corn cribs have slats, and the shucks of corn come through the spaces between the slats. So instead of spaces, our backsides were going to have so many stripes, we wouldn't hold shucks. He usually used his razor strap, and we were scared to death of that. When he gave us a thrashing, it lasted a long time. According to some psychologists today, I should've grown up to be a mass murderer because I got so many whippings, but I love Mama and Daddy for the whippings I got. Every one I got, I deserved.

When my Uncle Henry lived with us, he worked for the light company. Things were all right for a pretty good while, but he finally went back to drinking. He knew my daddy didn't allow alcohol in the house, so he caught a train out of town and we never saw him again. But Aunt Donna stayed around, and we still loved to get the candy she would bring.

I was up on our roof one day after it had been raining. It was a wood shingle roof, and those shingles were still slick from the rain. I saw Aunt Donna coming in the front gate, and when I started down, my feet flew out from under me and there I went down the roof of a

two-story house. I caught hold of the gutter, and I held on. The gutter was coming loose the whole time, but I finally got back up on the roof, and then I climbed down and got my candy.

We had a large room upstairs where the boys slept, and that room was great on a rainy day. We would play baseball, and we used a rolled-up magazine for our bat. The ball was a sock stuffed with other socks, and we used beds and furniture for our bases. We played up there all the time, and although we would fight other people, I don't remember getting in fights with my brothers at all. We had a solid family.

One of my very best childhood friends was Huddy Alexander. Huddy had infantile paralysis, which was later called polio, and he could walk a little bit, but only if he held onto something. We became friends in elementary school, and we stayed friends. He lived about three miles from us over on Liberty Pike. One of the highlights of going to Huddy's house happened one day when I was coming up by their spring. I saw this old mama skunk running toward a hole, and she had six little baby skunks right behind her. We called them polecats, and they were the cutest little things I ever saw. I ran just fast enough to keep the mama going to where the little ones couldn't quite keep up. She went in the hole, and I ran up and put a rock in the way so the babies couldn't get in. Then I took off my shirt and made me a knapsack out of it, and I put the skunks in it and carried them up to Huddy's house.

He came to the door and when I showed him those baby skunks, his eyes nearly popped out of his head. We played with them and played with them, and he finally said, "We should keep them for pets." I said, "No, they will stink when they get older." But he said he knew how to fix them. His daddy was a writer and his mother was an educated woman, so I thought he knew what he was talking about. If anybody came from that background, I just assumed he knew what he was talking about. So I said, "All right. How are you going to fix them?"

He told me to go upstairs to the bathroom and get his daddy's razor and some cotton balls and a can of ether they had. I brought it all back down, and right outside the kitchen door there was a big locust stump about three feet off the ground. It was perfect for an operating table. I thought I was going to watch him work

on the skunks, but he said I was doing it. He said he would tell me what to do. So he put one of them to sleep and handed him to me, and I started cutting. I didn't know what I was looking for, or why I was cutting in the places I was cutting. When the one I was working on died, he handed me another one. He'd say don't cut that way, cut this way. Well, most of them died on the operating table, but at least one of them got away and ran under the house and escaped, thank goodness.

One day I went over to visit Huddy, and we were riding ponies. He had a little Shetland pony, and I had to boost him up so he could get on. Then I got on a larger pony, and we trotted off down through the fields like we were cowboys. We ended up at this vacant tenant house. Whoever had lived there had left a corn-cob pipe on the mantle, and that gave us the idea of getting some corn silk to smoke. Well, we smoked some and then we got back

on the ponies again and started riding. Pretty soon we stopped, but the ground kept moving and kept bouncing. Then I started throwing up like crazy, and I never touched a cigarette again—ever.

Huddy had a hard time walking, but that didn't keep us from fishing when he came over to my house. I was pretty big, and I'd carry him on my back. I don't remember him being that heavy. So

I'd have Huddy on my back, and I'd follow the paths the cows had made on their way to the creek. We were always barefooted in the summer, and those paths made for easier walking on the way to our fishing hole. On the way we might see a tumblebug, or dung beetle, rolling along a dung ball. The ball would be pushed into a small hole so the encased eggs would hatch from the decaying dung. There were so many ways to learn about nature if you lived on a farm.

A creek ran in front of our house and we would go down there all the time. We'd fish or build dams. We'd get down in the water and put our hands on the bottom and kick our feet and say we were swimming. One time that got me in trouble.

Mrs. Helen Alexander, Huddy's mother, asked my mother if I could go with them down to Boyle, Mississippi. There were a lot of people at the lake down there, and some lady asked me, "Can you swim?" I said, "Yes ma'am." I didn't have a bathing suit, but Mrs. Alexander had given me an old one-piece woolen bathing suit that was a few sizes too big. Well, I couldn't swim, and that lake was about 50 feet deep.

We went down and there was a boat, and I held on the back of the boat and kicked my feet while the guys in the boat were rowing around the lake. As I was out there kicking, that old bathing suit got heavy and it began to slip down. I was scared. I couldn't turn loose to grab my bathing suit, and then I felt it fall off the end of my feet. About that time Mrs. Alexander said, "You

all come on in, it's time to eat." Well, I couldn't get out in front of all those girls and women, so I said, "I'm not hungry." Everybody else got out, and I was still in the water holding onto the boat. They kept saying, "Come on," and I kept saying, "I'm not hungry." Mrs. Alexander finally figured it out. She got a big towel and came down and held it around me while I got out of the water. It was the most

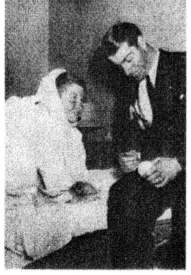

embarrassed I had ever been.

At the start of sixth grade, Huddy went up to New York City to have an operation to help his walking. He was gone for five months. I really missed him, and I was at the train station when he got back. Joe DiMaggio had come to the hospital in New York to meet Huddy, and I couldn't wait to shake the hand that had actually touched Joe DiMaggio.

Huddy with Joe DiMaggio.

We finally got a radio at our house. One day I was playing in the backyard and my mother came to the door and said, "I just heard over the radio that Will Rogers has been killed." I really didn't know who Will Rogers was, but I knew he must be a famous person. At night we would listen to "Amos and Andy" and "Ma Perkins" and a lot of those old radio shows.

We didn't have an automobile, but we got along pretty well. Mr. W. C. Yates, who taught and coached football at Franklin High School, and who was later superintendent of the county schools, lived across the road from us. Sometimes if it was bad weather and we needed to get somewhere, he would give us a ride in his car. He would also bring us ice. Huddy's mother and a lot of our neighbors put their food in a spring to keep it cold, but we used an icebox. Mr. Yates would usually come on Saturday afternoon from the icehouse in Franklin, and there would be a block of ice tied to the bumper of his car.

After supper we would get our Saturday night baths, which we usually got in a wash tub in the kitchen. We had to carry the water in from the pump outside. We had sulfur water, and it smelled awful, but that's what we had. And on Saturday nights during cold weather, when we couldn't go barefooted to church, Daddy would shine all of our shoes and line them up so they would be ready for us to put on the next morning.

On Sunday mornings in the summer, Daddy would make home-made ice cream from some of the ice that Mr. Yates had brought us. He would go out and turn the crank until the ice cream was ready. Sometimes we would be out there bothering him, and he would say,

"Wait a minute boys, let me give each one of you a chunk of ice."
They would be about the size
of a golf ball, and he'd tell
us to hold it in our hands.
Then he would put a little salt
on it and he would say,
"Hold it tight and see how
many times you can run
around the house before you
have to put it down." We would make four or five trips around the
house before our hands got so cold we would have to throw down
the ice. That was his way of getting us out of his hair.

Then he would cover the ice cream up while we went to
Sunday school and church. If it was good weather our whole family
would walk the mile and a half to the Fourth Avenue Church of
Christ, which was just off Main Street in Franklin. My brothers and
I went barefooted to church when it was warm enough. We only
had one pair of shoes each, and they had to last as long as they
could. If you wore out a hole in the bottom, you would cut out some
cardboard and put it in there to cover up the hole. You'd have to
change the cardboard every day or two. Later on, thank goodness,
they came out with linoleum, which lasted a long time.

I can remember sitting in a pew at church and swinging my
legs back and forth before they were long enough to reach the floor.
And I remember being so impressed with the older men in the church.

They would sit at the
end of the pew, and
when it came time for a
prayer, they would step
out into the aisle and get
down on one knee. You
don't see that any
longer. Then after

35

church we'd walk back home and eat our ice cream out in front of the house. There was nothing like eating ice cream on a hot day. And on summer nights, when it was too hot to sleep in the house, we would get blankets or a quilt and sleep on the porch, or go out and sleep under the big tree in the front yard.

September would come around, and we'd be walking back to school again. It was a mile from the corner of Ralston Lane and Murfreesboro Road, where we lived, to the old iron bridge over the Harpeth, and then another three-quarters of a mile or so to Franklin Elementary School. Our mother always told us to look out for a mad dog, but we never saw one. There wasn't much else to worry about. The only crime I remember was one night when somebody stole our chickens. Most people just didn't do things like that back then. There were a few bootleggers around, and that was it. We thought that maybe whoever had done it was hungry. Daddy just came in and said, "Our chickens are gone." We were proud of our chickens, and there went our whole flock—maybe 15 or 20.

After a few weeks of school, it would be Halloween. Halloween wasn't too big a holiday then—kids just went around causing problems for their neighbors. And then it would be Thanksgiving, and my mother would fix an even bigger meal than usual, with either a turkey or a big fat hen along with all the rest of the food she usually made. But what we really looked forward to was Christmas. Christmas Eve would come, and we would all get a chair and go in and sit in a semicircle in front of the fireplace. After we wrote our letters to Santa Claus, we would each put our letter over the fire. The rising heat would take it right up the chimney and, we thought, all the way to Santa. Then we each hung one of our socks on our chair, and after a while we'd finally go to bed. The next morning we got up early and ran down to see what Santa had brought us. Our socks would be stuffed with apples and oranges and hard candy. There might be a present or two, but we didn't expect much, and we appreciated anything we got.

Just after Christmas, 1937, I went up to Bowling Green, Kentucky, to visit my sister, Dorthy. I was in the sixth grade and it was only the second time I had been out of Tennessee. A phone call came late on the night of December 29. Daddy was dead. He had been at home sitting in a chair after supper, and he had just died. We left for home that same night. I had never been out traveling at night like that, and it was spooky and scary. I knew he was dead, but I was still expecting him to be all right when we got back. Everything seemed strange—there was a lot of fog—I was afraid. We got home around three in the morning.

Mr. Yates had come over and picked Daddy up out of the chair and put him on the bed. We didn't take his remains to a funeral home, so everything that was done with his body before the funeral was done at our house. I remember my mother gathering the children around the casket, and I remember her talking to Daddy. She said, "What you have left me with, these children, means more to me than all the gold in the world."

Several friends of the family brought their automobiles, and there was a small procession to Mount Hope Cemetery, where Daddy was buried. It was probably a month after his death before I realized he wasn't ever coming home.

Living off the Land

Chapter Four

When my daddy died, Mama was left with seven children to take care of. She didn't have any income, so she had to come up with the rent for the place, and with enough money to buy a few staples in the way of food. We knew that it had become our responsibility to bring Mama food for our family.

My brother Dan was seventeen years old when Daddy died, and I was twelve. We ended up pairing off, and although I had done a little hunting and trapping and fishing while Daddy was alive, I did those things almost every day after he was gone. Dan must have learned some of what he knew from Daddy, but he figured out a lot on his own, and then he taught it to me.

Not too many days went by that we didn't go out and catch rabbits with our hands. We didn't have a gun, so we would just go out without anything. It didn't take long to catch a rabbit. You can't outrun a rabbit, so we would just run him over to a rock fence. If he went up under the rocks, we put a rock in so he couldn't come back out the same hole he'd gone in. We'd go up to the top of the fence and start pulling away rocks until we could reach down and pick him up, and that's all there was to it. If we couldn't get to the

rabbit that way, we got a forked
stick and sharpened it, and then
we'd stick it in and twist it until we got the fur caught up,
and we'd just pull him out.
Sometimes we caught them
after a snow. We'd see a set of
tracks going into the brush pile
with no tracks coming out. We
would ease up, and all of a sudden we'd
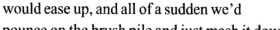
pounce on the brush pile and just mash it down like a web or a net so
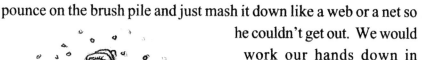
he couldn't get out. We would
work our hands down in
there and get him out, and
we did the same thing when
they hid in honeysuckle.
Catching rabbits was no
problem.

Our neighbor Mr.
Campbell had a wheat field, and Uncle Henry Poynter drove the
binder that cut the wheat. The area of uncut wheat would get smaller
and smaller, and the rabbits kept going to the middle. Then Uncle
Henry would say, "You boys get ready." We would have fishing
pole canes, and when we got close, the rabbits would try to run
away across the open stubble. We
would run the younger
rabbits down and hit
them with our poles. It
depended on how
many we wanted as to
how many we could
get in a day. Sometimes
when the wheat was being

cut, we could get 15 to 20 rabbits out of there, and then other times we would only get two or three for the family to eat.

Squirrels were pretty easy to catch, too. The squirrel would go up a tree and that is where I wanted him to go. He would go in a hole, and I would go up the tree behind him. I would take a forked stick or a piece of barbed wire and stick it in the hole. Then I'd twist it around until his tail got caught and just pull him out.

Of course, there was a whole lot more to feeding our family than catching rabbits and squirrels. We got milk from our cows and eggs from our chickens. Mama was a master when it came to wringing the neck of a chicken. Their bodies would keep hopping around after they were dead, and she would put a basket over them to keep them from going all over the yard. And we still had our garden. We grew potatoes, beans, corn, and tomatoes, along with the other usual garden vegetables. Mama did a lot of canning. There were always plenty of jars of vegetables and fruit in our cellar, and we would have that to eat throughout the winter. There were black-berry patches and a few pecan trees around, and we would also gather wild asparagus and poke sallet, so there was food out in the fields and in the woods. I don't ever recall us coming home without something for her to fix for supper.

Sometimes Mama would ask us to bring her some sassafras. We would find a red sassafras tree and follow the roots out near the surface of the ground, and once we found them, we'd dig down and cut off three or four of the roots. They would be a little bit bigger than a broomstick, and we took them down to the creek and swished off the dirt. Then we split them into little sections about two or three inches long, and Mama would put that in a pan with some boiling water and make sassafras tea.

The older we got, the better we were at getting food. We caught fish with our hands. The first time I did it was down in the creek in front of our house, but later on we'd catch them in the river. We had to go barefooted when we went to catch fish that way. You would walk through the water until you found a big rock, then you would take your foot and go around the edge of the rock until you found an opening. If that opening had some real fine silt pushed back outside and sort of mounded up a little bit, that told you there was a fish under there.

That old catfish had taken his tail and cleaned out the bed underneath the rock and pushed out all that silt. Then you'd go under the water and put your hand back under there.

The fish might not do anything, and if he didn't, you just sort of rubbed on him until you could work your thumb into his mouth.

Once you got your fingers in his gills, you had him. He might weigh anywhere from two to eight pounds. The teeth of a catfish are like sandpaper. If they bit you it didn't really hurt, although it was sort of surprising at first. But if you jerked your hand back you would scratch yourself, so we learned to just let them bite. We'd move our fingers into his mouth and just pull him out. We could catch five or six good catfish and bring them home, but that was only in the spring when they were bedding. We didn't have a refrigerator, so there wasn't any point in catching too many. They would bed under the same rock every year. It was just a matter of going down and getting them.

I didn't care for snakes. I was only bitten once, and it was my own fault. I was groping around for catfish under a riverbank instead of a rock. I reached back under the bank and a snake bit me on the finger, but it was just a water snake. I never saw a rattlesnake except in the western part of Williamson County.

Another way we got food was robbing the hives of wild honeybees. We were hungry, and we wanted that honey. If the tree wasn't too big, we would just cut it down with an ax. We would have that hive down close to the ground, and then we would build a fire underneath their opening, and the smoke would make them leave. We would usually take a washtub and put it under the hole. Then we would run our hands all the way in, and we would have honey all over our arms on up to our elbows. We might pull out twenty pounds of honey that way.

One time Dan and I went up the creek, and there was a swarm of bees that had gotten onto a low-hanging limb near the water. We wanted to take those bees home. We went back and got a box and a handsaw, and then we came back to get the bees. Dan was going to hold the limb on either side of the bees, and I was going to saw the branch off before he let the swarm drop into the box. We didn't have on anything to protect us at all. Well, while I was sawing, the bees were on him but they were not stinging. They were crawling

42

around on him, and just as I cut the limb free, a bee started to go up his nose. He was holding the branch with the bees all over it and he puffed out through his nose, and then the bee went down and stung him on his lip. Dan threw the whole swarm down into the box, and there was just an explosion of bees. We jumped off into the creek and got away, and we never did get those bees back to the house.

It wasn't too long before I started trying to make a little money by trapping animals for their pelts. My first venture in trapping didn't turn out too well. I set a trap in a hole under Mrs. Johnson's barn, and when I came by the next morning, I pulled the trap out to see what I had caught. I was sprayed full blast by a polecat. When I got home, my mother made me hang my clothes on the clothesline and build a fire with green cedar branches to smoke out some of the odor. At school the next day the classroom was very hot, which made matters worse. My teacher, Miss Josephine Wirt, smelled something. She stood up and started walking up and down each row. When she finally got to me she said, "Jimmy, go home!"

Most of what I learned about trapping came from my brother Dan. We usually trapped muskrat or mink. Creeks were the best places to trap, and the best trapping creek of them all was Spencer Creek, a little north of Franklin. We would walk along through the water and look for telltale signs. There would be footprints, and muskrats would make long slick places where they slid down the bank and into the water. And there might be paths back under the roots of trees, or some mussel shells they had pried open, or mock oranges they had eaten. Muskrats like to be where there is lots of vegetation and the mink were there too, because the mink preyed on the muskrat.

We caught them in steel traps. We would put the traps back under the bank and have them staked out in the deep water. We didn't bait the traps, because if we baited them it would've brought in dogs and cats and everything else. When the trap sprung, the animal would try to swim away and go down in the deep water, but the trap would weigh him down and he would drown. We would go out just as it began to get daylight, and we'd run our traps and bring in our catch. When we first started out, we probably didn't catch over three or four mink a year, and maybe fifteen or twenty muskrat.

We had to skin and dry the pelts, and then we'd sell them to Mr. Martin Tohrner, who had a place right across from the icehouse. Mr. Tohrner would grade our furs and then pay us. Mink was the prize, because even though it was the Depression, a mink pelt could bring $25. That was big money back then. A good muskrat pelt would bring two or three dollars. A black guy named John Henry worked there, and he would take the pelts up a ladder and throw them into a little loft. I always wanted to go up there and see how much fur he had. I depended on the money I made to buy clothes. All the clothes I wore from seventh grade on, I paid for myself by selling fur.

One of the nicest men I have ever known was Henry Cannon. He was a family friend. The house that I was born in belonged to his family. Later on he would marry Sarah Colley, who was better known as Minnie Pearl. Some time before World War II he joined the Army. He was going to leave, so he let us have his 20-gauge shotgun. So we finally had a shotgun. I wasn't quite ready for a shotgun, but one day my brother Dan and a friend of his came along, and his friend had a 12-gauge shotgun. They wanted to see how I would handle the kick I would get if I shot it. I was scared. I didn't want to do it, but Dan's friend said he would put his hat down and let me shoot it. I remember shooting his hat, and the kick of that gun nearly knocked me down, but from that day on I liked hunting with a shotgun.

Dan and Campbell Haffner were good friends, and they hunted together. They only had one shotgun, so one would get to shoot three times, and then the other one got three shots. They were out hunting one day and it was Dan's turn to shoot. Campbell flushed a covey of quail, and somehow or other Dan shot Campbell. I was sitting on a fence post in our backyard when I saw Dan coming across the field carrying Campbell over his shoulder. He yelled to me to tell Mama to call a doctor. When they got close, I could see the blood. Doctor Dan German came and pulled the pieces of shot out of Campbell's face and shoulders. Fortunately his eyes were okay. Ever since then, Dan has been called Shotgun Gentry.

Having that gun made it a lot easier to kill rabbits and squirrels and possums. Those were about all we hunted since there weren't any deer around back then. I never saw a deer when I was growing up. Shooting was easy, but I could still hunt with my hands, and one time that got me in trouble. I was hunting by myself up on Pritchard's Bluff, out north of Lewisburg Pike, and a little sleet was falling. A squirrel ran up a tree and I had the shotgun with me, but I couldn't get a good shot at him. I only had two or three shells, and I didn't want to waste a shot. So I went out and grabbed a low-hanging branch and pulled it down. I threw my leg around it and climbed up to the trunk of the tree, and then I went up from there.

Well as I went up, the squirrel went up, and as he went higher, I went higher, too. I got to where I was standing on one limb, but I couldn't quite reach the next limb. But I wanted that squirrel, so I jumped up and grabbed the next limb and held on, even though it was slick. I had a little hatchet with me, and the squirrel decided he had to come down because he couldn't go any higher. He started down, and when he did I hit him with my hatchet and he fell out of the tree. I was thirty or forty feet up in the air, and I realized I had to go back down to a limb I couldn't quite reach. I finally just said, "Okay, here I go," and I let go. I think I went around that limb three or four times trying to hold on. How I kept from falling I do not know.

I was young when I started using a shotgun, but I guess I had already learned how to shoot and how to be careful. We had already been making weapons on our own. We would take the tongue out of an old shoe, and cut it so we could put a rubber band through it. That made a good gravel shooter, which was different from a slingshot. We could hit birds with it and lots of other things. Some boys would shoot the insulators off the electrical wires up on the pole with rocks. We got pretty skilled at shooting those things.

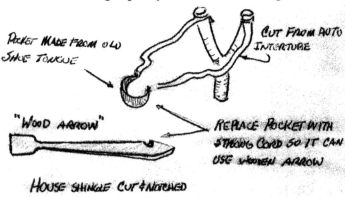

POCKET MADE FROM OLD SHOE TONGUE

CUT FROM AUTO INTERTUBE

"WOOD ARROW"

REPLACE POCKET WITH STRONG CORD SO IT CAN USE WOODEN ARROW

HOUSE SHINGLE CUT & NOTCHED

We made something out of wooden roof shingles that was much more dangerous. The shingle would be tapered—heavy on one end and thin on the opposite end. We would cut the shingle in an inch-and-a-half wide strip and bring it to a point on one end. Then we would cut a notch in the heavy end and taper it back like an arrow. We hooked that on a string, and we could shoot those things out of sight. Then we made them even more dangerous and deadly by putting a nail on the end. We made other things beside weapons. We also made scooters out of discarded skates. We took a two by four and nailed wheels on the front and back, and then we nailed on an upright for the handlebars.

We did a lot of hunting and fishing and trapping, but we still did a lot of playing. We would cool down on hot summer days by taking a dip in the Harpeth. Sometimes somebody would take our clothes while we were swimming, and although we could always find them somewhere nearby, they had usually been put in the water and then tied up in knots. If the river flooded in the summertime, we would go upstream and find an old log and roll it off into the water. Then we'd jump in and just ride the log back down the river.

SCHOOL DAYS AND MAMA

Chapter Five

With each September would come another school year. I can remember almost all of my elementary teachers. Mrs. Josephine Wirt could write either left or right handed. And there was Mrs. Sallie Seay, Mrs. Jessie Gray, Mrs. Ethel Jones, and Mr. Haun. We would call him Mr. Horn, and say, "Ole Jake Horn with his belly full of corn." We thought he was the oldest man around, but he insulted us by saying any baseball we could throw to him, he could catch barehanded. We thought we could really throw hard, but he caught everything we threw. We would never see him smile. We were scared of Mr. Haun, but he was a good man.

I would take my lunch to school wrapped in newspaper, and everybody else did, too. All those lunches looked pretty much the same. Sometimes boys would find out who had the best lunches, and move all the lunches around so nobody knew which one was which. Only the ones who had done it knew where the best food was, and they ended up with the best lunches.

In those days there weren't too many students, and in the fall a doctor examined every child in the county. They would look for things like cavities, bad teeth, poor eyesight, skin rashes, weight problems, and they would keep a record. They would come back in the early spring and recheck the students, and if all the problems had been corrected, then that child got a blue ribbon. On Blue Ribbon Day everybody wore a white shirt and their ribbon. They would have a big parade down Main Street in Franklin, and it would end up at the high school where they could watch all the running and jumping and throwing going on at Field Day. Blue Ribbon Day was a big day for us.

One day Huddy Alexander saw me draw something on paper, and when he told me how good it was, that encouraged me. Close to the end of elementary school there was a contest for drawing, and Mrs. Caroline Bell got me to enter. I won first place and got a $10 prize. That really got me started with my drawing. We didn't have any art in school, and I think if I had gotten into it early enough, I could have really done something with it by now.

I didn't mind school, but I had gotten more and more interested in athletics. By seventh and eighth grade we had moved

Franklin Elementary School, November 1936
My Principal was Mr. Haun and my teacher was Mrs. Wirt. Rebecca
is the seventh student in the first row. Huddy is the sixth student in
the third row. I'm the seventh student in the fifth row.

49

to the back part of the playground, where we would play football and baseball during recess. We couldn't see the girls because the building blocked our view, but we thought that real boys didn't want to be seen near girls anyway. But by the time my friends and I promoted ourselves to the back of the playground, I knew the names of at least two girls. One was Mary Williams, the best student in school, and the other was Rebecca Channell.

I wanted to play football on a team, and we finally got ourselves organized. We didn't get a coach until Fred Isaacs, one of the players at the high school, hurt his leg and volunteered to be our coach. It might have been our neighbor, Mr. Yates, who let me have some old white hand-me-down jerseys from the high school. I took them home, and all Mama had was black dye, so she dyed them all black and we painted white numbers on the back. We were so proud of those jerseys. During eighth grade we won every game we played, and we had to cut our season short because we couldn't find anyone else who would play us. I was pretty big and Mr. Charles Oliver, the coach of the high school, asked me to play on the high school team for the rest of the season. I played tackle and I only had street shoes, and I remember how I couldn't get any traction. Those high school guys with cleats on would just slide me backward off the line of scrimmage.

That same year we got up a basketball team. We didn't have a coach, and we started our season with one of our teachers, Miss Ethel Jones, taking us to games in her car. We loved Miss Ethel for showing an interest in our team, but she embarrassed us by using bobby pins to keep the hair out of our eyes. And we didn't like to wear shorts—we thought that only sissies wore shorts. Finally Vernon Beard, another high school student, became our coach, and we went on to have a great season. We found out we were not the best team around because a team from Cheatham County, called Bear Wallow, killed us. It was something like Bear Wallow 18 and Franklin Elementary 12. We didn't know exactly where Bear

Wallow was or how old their guys were, but they were bigger than we were, and we saw them out taking a smoke after the game.

There were only two gymnasiums in Franklin, and they were both very small. At BGA the basket was actually on the wall. If you went under the basket for a shot, you had to stop, because if you didn't, you would hit the wall. Franklin's gym was not much bigger, and neither were the ones out in Hillsboro and College Grove. So we did most of our practicing on outdoor courts, but we played a lot more baseball and football back then anyway.

After school we used to go behind the courthouse where the water tank was located. Since the ground had to be smooth, it was the best place around to shoot marbles. We would draw a big circle and play marbles with some of the town boys before we went home. We also shot  marbles at school, and even though we weren't supposed to shoot for keeps, we did anyway. We wanted to win all the marbles away from the other guy. One time Mama found out I had kept somebody's marbles, and I ended up getting a switching.

We played marbles more than anything else, but we also used to play mumbly peg a lot. You play mumbly peg with a pocket-knife. The idea is to flip the knife in all sorts of different ways—off your palm, off the back of your hand, over your shoulder—and have it stick in the ground. Whoever won got to find a little stick, which was

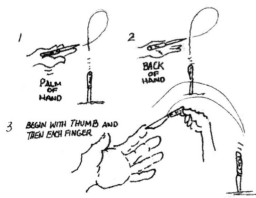

whittled down and sharpened into a peg. Then the peg was pushed down into the dirt, and whoever lost had to get down and pull it up, just using his teeth.

I missed my daddy, but Mama did everything for our family. She fed us, she cleaned for us, she disciplined us and, when we needed it, she would console each and every member of our family. What more could a mother do than show us that her family was her life? Sometimes she would give us a nickel tied up in a handkerchief so we wouldn't lose it, and we'd go in to town and buy candy.

The lessons we learned from Mama did not come from a book. They came from her heart. She taught respect for others by never criticizing or saying anything derogatory about any individual. I never heard her say anything bad about anybody. She showed kindness to those people who it would have been easy to find fault with. Respect was practiced at our house by standing when a guest entered the room. We were taught to show respect to our elders by saying, "Yes ma'am", "no ma'am", "yes sir", and "no sir". We didn't talk when adults were talking. We were taught that you took your manners with you to school, to church, and to someone's house. On a bus you always stood and offered your seat to a lady. You helped your date with her chair in a restaurant. In a public place you removed your hat to show respect to a person, or to some place or thing of honor. You never took the last biscuit. You helped those with little or no food. You said you were sorry when you did something wrong. Those were good, homemade lessons from a mother who had little if any formal education. Her God-given motherly instincts were what guided our family through the Depression years of the 1930s.

There was not a lot of hugging in our family. Mama never did that. She couldn't get around to all of us at once. But she didn't have to tell us she loved us—we knew she did. I would say the same prayer every night when I went to bed:

> Now I lay me down to sleep.
> I pray the Lord my soul to keep.
> If I should die before I wake,
> I pray the Lord my soul to take. Amen.

Mama would always be kneeling beside the bed, and when I had finished my prayer, she would bend down and kiss me on the forehead.

Some of those nights got pretty cold. We had a wash bowl in our room, and sometimes the water would freeze overnight. But I don't remember being too cold. There were usually three of us in bed together, and we'd just cover ourselves up with more quilts. When it really got cold, we would heat a brick in the fireplace, and then wrap it in a cloth and put it in the bed with us. When we would have a good snow, Mama would tell one of us to go out and bring her a scoop of it. She would add sugar and milk and vanilla flavoring, and we would have snow ice cream. I ate it so fast I would get a headache, and I learned a good lesson from that.

We loved the snow. The snow meant hunting and snow ice cream, and when the Harpeth would freeze a bunch of us would go down to the river. We would get out on the ice and say we were skating. But we didn't have any skates, just our leather shoes. Sometimes we'd build a fire out on the ice, and later on some idiot might shoot a hole to see if he could break through it. If it started cracking, everybody would run for their lives. We didn't do much sledding because we didn't have any sleds. We didn't have boots to amount to anything, so we would wrap our feet in burlap bags when we were going to stay out in the snow for very long. We always looked forward to snows.

Christmas was different after Daddy was gone, but we still looked forward to it. My brother Dan was always sort of a prankster and a fun maker. The only heat in the house was the fireplace, and one Christmas Eve we were all sitting around the fire. When it was almost time to go to bed, Dan said to Mama, "Santa Claus didn't bring me anything last year. I'm going to get my shotgun and kill him tonight." He got  up and got the shotgun out of the corner. When he did, we started crying and holding onto him while he dragged us across the floor. Mama, who was in on the joke, finally talked him into putting the shotgun down. The next morning each of the younger children had gotten a new pair of bib overalls, a red bandana, and a pack of firecrackers, along with the fruit and candy in our socks. Dan was pretending to cry. He had a shoebox full of ashes and switches in his lap, and we tried to make him feel better by offering him some of our candy.

Town and country

Chapter Six

In 1939 we moved back into town, into a house on Fifth Avenue.

The day we left our place on Murfreesboro Road was one of the worst days of my life, but once we got settled I realized the country was still close by. All I had to do was walk one block over to Fourth Avenue, then across the railroad track to the Harpeth River. We

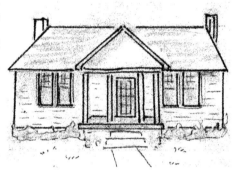

continued to hunt and fish and trap like before. Living so near the

Harpeth, it wasn't long before I decided to build a boat. I got some cypress from Mr. Harvel Hughes' lumber yard, and I built the boat down at Dead End, where Fourth Avenue stopped at the river.

Huddy Alexander, E. T. Johnson, and I got together enough supplies to last several days, and then we paddled about five miles up the river to a nice grassy spot on the south side of the water under some shade trees. We set up our tent, and while Huddy and I got ready to do some cooking, E. T. took his .22 rifle and went across the river. Soon we heard a rifle shot, and E. T. showed up and said he had shot a goose. The  owner of the goose had also heard the shot, and pretty soon he showed up, too. It was Mr. Gordon McDaniel, and he said not to shoot the rifle anymore, and he left. Not long after that, a water snake swam out from under the bank where we were, and E. T. shot at the snake. That brought back Mr. McDaniel, and he was mad. He said he was going to call the police. We took down the tent as fast as we could, threw everything we had into the boat, and headed back. The whole way back we worried that the law would be waiting for us when we got home.

When we moved to town, I made some new friends. One day it had rained pretty heavily, so we went over and dammed up the drainage ditch on Cummins Street behind the Farnsworth Lumber Company. We were having the best time, but all of a sudden Mr. Oscar Garner came up in his police car and climbed out and, boy, he got on us. Our dam had backed the water up into Mrs. Ragsdale's grocery store, which was up on the corner of Cummins and Margin Street. Mr. Garner told us to tear it down, and he said, "You boys come see the judge in the morning at the courthouse." Well, it scared the daylights out of me. I went home and told Mama.

The next morning she got me all cleaned up and got my hair pasted down good, and I was probably cleaner than I had ever been in my life. I remember going down Main Street and Mr. Garner was on the square directing traffic. He saw me and he said, "You are Zeb's boy, aren't you? I won't say anything to the judge about you, but those other boys have been giving us a lot of trouble." He said, "You be careful who you run with," and I went back home. That made a big impression on me.

My brother and I were still going out and getting food for our family. Dan and I learned to catch catfish by limb lining. We would find a low-hanging branch over the water, and we'd tie a line on it with a single hook. The key was the kind of bait we used—live minnows. Some people tried to use things like liver. When they did that, they caught things like turtles or old mudcats. There was a certain kind of minnow we always used called a bullmouth or creek chub, and there was another one called a steelback. If they were good and alive when we put them on the hook, they would swim around about three or four inches down, and as they swam they attracted catfish, especially the forked-tail blue catfish, which we called bluecats. We loved to catch those.

We would put the lines out just before dark, and most of the time we would stay all night. We would sleep until daybreak, and then we would run them again and take our lines up. When we saw the tree branch dipping down, we knew we had one. We might put out as many as 100 lines, and we would probably catch fish on half the lines we put out. It was a great way to catch fish.

One time Dan and I decided we'd go out and hunt frogs all night long. We waded into the water up at the Epworth Church at Millview, which was about seven miles up river from the bridge on Murfreesboro Road, and then we started down the river. We would find them with our flashlights. We could hear them up ahead, and when we shined our lights around in the darkness, there they were. Underneath their bottom jaw would show white, and their eyes would glare a little bit. We'd just ease over in the water real close and then grab them. It took quick hands. You didn't have much chance if you missed them the first time.

But there were so many of them, that you didn't worry about the ones you missed, because there would be another one a few feet farther on. We'd stuff them into a tow sack, and there would be frogs jumping all over the place in there. By the time we got down to where the city reservoir in Franklin is now, we were worn out. We had somewhere between seventy-five and one hundred big frogs. We got out of the water just at day- break and we found a long pole. We tied the bag over the pole, and put one end of the pole on Dan's shoulder and one end on mine, and then we walked home.

So after we moved to town, we still had places to play, we still hunted and fished, and of course, we still had school. I enjoyed school, but I didn't study. I should have studied more, but back then catching rabbits and squirrels, fishing, and doing all those other things were my priorities. But I didn't mind going to school.

In 1940 I entered Franklin High School as a freshman. I had briefly been a member of the football team the year before, but it was my first time to be a student there. Mr. W. C. Yates, who had been our neighbor out on Murfreesboro Road, had become head coach. I really looked up to Mr. Yates. He had helped fill part of the gap that was made by the death of my father. Mr. Yates was dedi- cated to the profession of teaching and coaching, and later on he influenced me to get into teaching and coaching. That freshman year we were playing Clarksville, and they had a big old boy I was supposed to block. He annihilated me at first, but I finally figured out a way to block him. When Mr. Yates congratulated me, I felt like I was nine feet tall.

Mr. Daly Thompson, the principal of the high school, was a great man and a real disciplinarian. He was a veteran of World War I. He didn't hesitate grabbing a boy and shaking him. He could get a boy's attention right fast if a boy didn't do what he said. Mr. Thompson was a great person. He would read the Bible every day in assembly, and he didn't want anybody talking while he was reading the Bible.

My main courses were general science, math, english, social studies, and history. Some boys would take shop, and some would take agriculture courses to prepare them to be farmers. I had no idea what I would end up doing with my life. Football was my long suit. I weighed about 185 pounds, so I was a pretty good-sized boy for back then. Both my brother Dan and my brother David had played high school football, and that added to my desire to play. I think my background made me aggressive. I believe it came from hunting and being in a large family. When I played, I played hard and I played to win. I also grew to appreciate baseball more and more because it was a relaxed game and it was more fun to play. I liked center field more than any other position, but I ended up playing first base and pitching a lot. I also played basketball, but overall, nothing topped football.

FRANKLIN AND WILLOW PLUNGE

Chapter Seven

Pretty soon we were all getting jobs so we could make some extra money. My older brother David worked at Gray's drugstore, and my younger brother Bobby worked at the movie house on Main Street and at Willow Plunge, a very popular swimming and recreation area out on Lewisburg Pike.

I got a job with the Colonial Bread Company. A driver would come out from Nashville before dawn and put the bread in a big wooden box with a padlock on it. When I came along at about six in the morning, the town would just be waking up. Almost every business in Franklin was along Main Street. There were at least eight  groceries, a meat market, a bakery, three automobile dealerships, three drugstores, the movie theatre, two pie wagons, and also doctors offices, clothing stores, and several churches.

I liked being in Franklin early in the morning. Two black men would come down Main Street not long after sunrise, walking along beside a two-wheeled cart pulled by a horse. The men had push brooms, and they would push up piles of trash and manure and put

it into the cart. I would unlock the box and take bread to H. G. Hill's store and to Dugger Ahearn's on the corner at Five Points. Before I got to the square there were M. P. Brothers', the Piggly Wiggly, Jennette's, and Ed Thurman's. And on the square there were Crockett's and Waggoner's, and C. P. Daniel's store was on East Main.

Back in those days customers would come in with a list, or they would just tell one of the clerks what they wanted to buy. The clerk would go back and get the

H. G. Hills Store
Lloyd Cook, Raymond Harper, Ed Thurman,
George Giles, Baxter Ewing, Paul Spencer.

items, and bring them up to the counter where the customer was waiting. I might put a total of 100 loaves of bread in those stores, and it would take me about thirty minutes. I worked six days for $2 a week, and I felt lucky to have the job. I would make my last delivery, and then go right on up Columbia Pike to the high school.

If I didn't have football or basketball or baseball after school, I might go back down to one of the drugstores on Main Street and see what was going on. People would play practical jokes from time to time. One of them would happen on Main Street, in front of Lunn and Garner's shoe store. Somebody would cut off the corner of a $20 bill, and have it sticking out of a wallet so that it looked like the wallet was full of money. The wallet was fastened to a wire, and the wire ran down through a manhole cover and was attached to a cowbell. The wallet was really wired up, and it wouldn't come loose.

We would sit around and watch the way people reacted when they came down the street. Somebody would see it and then turn around, walk back real fast, and pick it up. It would nearly break their arms when they did that. Others would look all around and then kneel down and get it. One lady stopped and was talking to another lady, and she backed up and put her foot over it so the other one wouldn't see it. Then when the second lady left, the first one tried to pick it up. Half of those who had the joke played on them would go across the street and watch the other fools come along and try to pick up the wallet.

Sometimes it was hard to walk through town on Saturday afternoons. You would have to go out into the street to get around people who had stopped to talk to each other on the sidewalk. The rock fence that ran on two sides of the Presbyterian Church furnished a resting place for the men who were waiting for their wives to finish shopping on Main Street. They would sit there and count the out-of-state cars that passed by, and there would be lots of pickup trucks with people sitting in chairs in the back on their way to see the Grand Ole Opry in Nashville.

One of the best known people in Franklin was a man named Fred Buford. Fred was unusual. Fred was a bit slow, and on Sundays he would go from church to church, and sometimes he would talk out loud to the preacher during the sermon. He would sell pencils and things like that on the sidewalk, and a lot of times he said embarrassing things to people. Years later when he was getting older, he was in the hospital and his black nurse told him she needed to give him a bath. He said, "Ain't no colored woman going to give me a bath." Of course, he didn't address her exactly that way. She said, "Mr. Buford, I won't enjoy it any more than you do." So Fred said, "Well, if you won't enjoy it, then go ahead and do it."

Franklin had another well-known individual named Si Kelton, but he was a lot more industrious than Fred Buford. Si was a black man who was in the business of building outdoor privies. When a prospective customer asked the price of one of his privies, Si would say a single hole model was $20, and the  "conversational model," which had two holes, was $35.

People knew each other in Franklin. When you walked down the street in those days, there was a lot of visiting. You might say, "How are you, Mrs. Harper?" And she'd say, "I'm doing fine. How about your mama? How's she doing?" And you'd talk for awhile.

One night we were at the corner of Margin and Fourth Avenue where Mrs. Whitfield lived, and she saw us. She said, "Are you boys going fishing tomorrow?" We said, "Yes ma'am, we probably will." She said, "Well, if you catch any fish, I want some." We caught some, and when we brought the fish to her, she asked what kind they were. Somebody said they were bugle mouth bass. That was another name for an old hogsucker, and whatever you call them, they are not fit to eat. It is about like eating briars. But she paid us 15 or 20 cents for them, so I guess she ended up trying to eat bugle mouth bass.

Franklin was a very close-knit place. Everybody knew everybody else. If you dialed 8, you got Mr. S. E. Farnsworth's lumberyard. If you dialed 45, you got the ice company. Our number was 477. Lillian Wauford was one of the operators in the telephone company office, which was right on the corner across from the post office. I'd call and say, "Lillian, please give me number 39." And she'd say, "Jimmy, they're not at home. They have gone to the grocery store." Or we would call Lillian and say we would like to go hunting or fishing in the morning, and she would call us at about 4:30 a.m. We would pick up the phone the next morning and she'd say, "It's time to go fishing." One morning she called and said, "Jimmy, E. T. said he would meet you at Liberty Pike and Ralston Lane." And this was all on the telephone. One time somebody made a call and Lillian said, "He's not at home, but I just saw him go down the street a minute ago." Everybody knew everybody else. Sometimes Harry Smith, the postman, would be reading the postcards he was delivering when the owner came to the door. He might reach out with a card and say, "Your sister is coming to see you next week."

In the summertime, back when we had lived on Lewisburg Pike, lines of cars would drive past our house on the way to Willow Plunge, which was just down the road going out of town. When we lived out on Murfreesboro Road and the wind was blowing from the south in June or July or August, we could hear the music from Willow Plunge. My brother Dan had started working there before we moved to town, then my brother Bobby and I started working there, too.

Mr. C. H. Kinnard built Willow Plunge back in the 1920s. He had used a mule and a scoop to dig out a place where his boys could play in the water. So many people got to coming out from town that he just made it bigger. He finally poured a concrete pool, and he gradually turned it into a fabulous place. The spring was about a quarter mile away, and he captured the water in pipes that ran into the two pools he eventually had.

Willow Plunge got its name from the willow trees that grew beside the pools. Their branches almost hung down to the water. The grass on the hillside was manicured like the greens on a golf course. There was a stand for soft drinks, and a coffee shop for hamburgers and french fries. Mrs. Tom Robinson and Mrs. Lacy Doss made chess pies, and there was a lot of other great food. There was a miniature golf course, and up on top of the hill, where there were plenty of shade trees, there was a pavilion for picnics.

I started off picking up trash and cutting the grass. I would cut the grass every morning with a push mower, and then I worked my way up to being a lifeguard. It was not unusual on a hot weekend afternoon for over 1500 people to be at Willow Plunge. Most of them wouldn't be swimming, they would be laying out in the sun getting a tan.

Mr. Kinnard would not allow any alcohol there—zero. If he suspected someone was drinking or bringing it in, he or the manager would say, "Get your things and leave now." There was no horseplay allowed, and boys and girls weren't permitted to neck. I don't ever recall seeing any fights. Except for someone trying to bring in alcohol, the worst thing that would happen was somebody trying to sneak in. It probably didn't cost but about 35 cents to get in. It was a wonderful place to go.

A WORLD OF CHANGE

Chapter Eight

We didn't hear much about the outside world in those days. I'd hear somebody talking about politics, or maybe there would be talk about what somebody had read in the newspaper. I knew there was a world out there, but I was so involved in the world around me, that I never thought much about what was going on out past the horizon.

On Sundays at Fourth Avenue Church of Christ there would always be a short break between Sunday School and church. White's Drugstore was the only place open on Sunday. Nine days after I turned sixteen I was at church, and we had walked around the corner to get a Coke. A bunch of us were standing around talking and the radio was on, and then someone yelled for everybody to be quiet. We listened to how the Japanese had bombed Pearl Harbor, and how a

lot of people had been killed. I still remember the shape of that radio. I can see it right now. We didn't say a word. We just put down our unfinished cokes and walked out. We knew right then that we were at war.

Guys who were only two or three years older than I was, guys I'd gone to school with, were soon going into the service. I admired  them. I wanted to be like they were. When a man went into the military, his mother, or his wife if he had one, would put a blue star in the window to represent that soldier. Some houses would have three or four stars in the window. There was talk about the war every day. We'd read about it in the newspaper. Guys were leaving to fight all the time, and I knew my time was coming.

It wasn't long before rationing started, and the older people were showing their patriotism by doing things like growing victory gardens and buying war bonds. Soldiers would come home on furlough, and I saw more and more guys in uniform on Main Street. A lot of us who were still in school were involved in gathering scrap iron to help the war effort. We also began to do some military drilling at the high school. I think we wore khaki pants and matching shirts, and we had student officers to lead the marching.

My brother David was two years ahead of me in school. He was smaller than I was and he had sandy red hair. David wasn't interested in the outdoors, but he was a very good athlete. He played football, basketball, and baseball for Franklin High School, and he and I were teammates when he was a junior and senior. He was a pretty good student, and he had a good sense of humor along with a sense of independence. He was sociable and well groomed, and that helped him in his job at Gray's Drugstore. David graduated from the high school less than six months after Pearl Harbor, and he went off to college at the University of Tennessee at Martin, but he couldn't wait to join the army.

Dan, David, me, William, and Bobby

When David was home he worked in the drugstore, and he wore a long white apron. He would go to work, but he kept trying to enlist. He didn't get in at first, then one day he walked down to the recruiting station, still wearing his apron, and there was an opening. He ran back to the drug store, turned in his apron, and asked Mr. Gray to give whatever money he was owed to Mama. Then he ran up the street and told her he was leaving. After that he got on the bus, and he was gone.

The war had changed a lot of things, but there was still hunting and fishing and trapping and school and sports. I was the captain of our football team as a junior and senior, and I played linebacker and fullback. Our offense was the single wing, so we didn't have a quarterback lined up behind the center. We had a blocking back, a fullback, a tailback, and a wingback, and with our system the fullback did all the passing. My favorite receiver was Pack Roberts. He was tall, and I liked to throw long to him. I learned some basic things about football from playing in high school. From a technique standpoint, I learned that if your body angles are wrong, you won't have any power. It was a matter of trial and error, but I learned to stay low and to keep my back straight. We did a whole lot of blocking and tackling back then, and I had plenty of chances to work on my form.

I had a pretty good junior year, and before the start of my senior year Mr. George Briggs, the headmaster of Battle Ground Academy, called Mama and asked if I could ride with him down to Leighton, Alabama. So I went down and met a boy named Henderson King, who was interested in coming to BGA. Mr. Briggs introduced me as the BGA captain for the coming year. I thought I had misunderstood him, but I hadn't. King ended up coming to BGA, and he turned out to be a good player. By the time we got back to Franklin, I thought I was going to BGA. I went home and when I told my mother, she said I would have to tell Mr. Thompson and Mr. Yates. When I went to tell them they said, "We don't see how you can do that," and in the end I couldn't see how I could do it either. So I stayed at Franklin.

Our biggest rivals were Shelbyville, Columbia, Springfield, Clarksville, and Mount Pleasant. Our home field was about a foot and a half lower on the west than it was on the east, so sometimes we were going uphill and sometimes we were going downhill. We had wooden bleachers, and on real cold nights some of the fans might break down part of the bleachers and build a fire, and then they'd stand beside the fire and watch the game.

One time we were playing a game against Mount Juliet. Lord it was bad blood. We had a couple of guys on our team who knew a couple of the guys on their team, and there was fighting almost every play. Finally somebody turned out the lights. Everything went dark, then it was whop, whop, whop. There were more hard licks passed in the dark than went on during the game. Finally the lights came back on, and the ball was gone. We didn't know where it was. The guys on the sidelines holding the chains had gone running for their lives.

Mr. Yates was our coach, and sometimes he would get us fired up for a game. Coaches didn't do a whole lot of that back then, but he did it some. We might not have known as many techniques as some other teams did, but we respected him and he got us ready to play.

71

Back then there was not much pressure on the coaches and the players. There wasn't a lot of lifting weights, and we didn't train year-round. We just showed up on the first day of practice, put on our uniforms, and started getting ready for the season. It was fun. I still had time to hunt and fish and do all the other things I enjoyed. I didn't know very much about professional or college sports. The only college players I knew much about were Harry Guffee and Pete Gracey, who both played at BGA and had gone on to play at Vanderbilt.

I had been selected most valuable player of the football team when I was a junior, and also when I was a senior. There was a banquet, and I knew I would have to stand up in front of people and get an award. The day of the banquet Mr. Yates said, "Now, Jimmy, don't forget tonight." I said, "Yes, sir," but I didn't end up going. I was just too timid.

1943 Franklin High School Football Team. I was number 43.

I was an introvert. I tried to stay unseen as much as I could. Girls did not have a place in my life. I was happy the way I was, and I didn't get involved with girls. But ever since second grade I had been noticing Rebecca Channell. I thought she was the prettiest girl who had ever lived, and a lot of other people thought so, too. She had plenty of boyfriends. We had been in school together all the way up into high school, but she had usually been in the smart class, and I'd usually been in the dumb class. I didn't talk to her, and if I saw her coming I would go the other way.

Rebecca

I saw her at school, and since I was a lifeguard, I saw her at Willow Plunge during the summer. She would show up with whatever boy she had a date with, and I would wish I was the one with her, or that she would come over and talk to me. Things went along like that until the spring of 1943, toward the end of our junior year. Then she wrote me a note that came out of the blue. We were in class together in the high school chemistry lab. Rebecca passed the note to somebody, and that person passed it on to me. The note simply said, "Will you go to the junior-senior prom with me?", signed Rebecca Channell. Up to that point I not only had never had a date with a girl, I don't remember having a lengthy conversation with a girl. But I wrote "OK" on the note, and I passed it back without looking in her direction.

The anticipation of catching a big fish, trapping a mink, or scoring a game-winning touchdown in a crucial game was nothing compared to the anticipation I felt about prom night. While I wanted to be with her more than anything in the world, I was afraid of not knowing what to say or how to act. I didn't know how to dance, and I was afraid she would be sorry she'd ended up going with me. Of course, I didn't have a car so we rode with Alex Moran, who was a classmate of mine, and his date. He drove up in an old A-Model Ford, and there was only seating for three. On the way to pick her up I worried about how four of us would fit into his car. Rebecca

73

lived at the corner of Fourth Avenue and Bridge Street, and her mother answered the door. She invited me in, and I probably just stood around and fidgeted. When Rebecca entered the room, I think I came out with something original like "Hi," and then I opened the door to leave. The size of the car gave me no choice but to have her sit on my lap. Thank goodness she knew the other couple, and they talked. I didn't know what to do with my hands, and I just stared straight ahead for the five or six block drive to the school. That drive seemed much longer than five or six blocks.

The gym was dark enough to make me feel like everyone was not looking at me, but then I saw my little brother Bobby and couple of others peeping in to see how I was doing. We finally danced, and I only stepped on her toes once. It was like I was dreaming. I had heard enough boys talk about dating to get the idea that I should try to get a goodnight kiss. When I walked her up to her house I didn't want to offend her, so I asked her for a kiss. She responded with a quick peck on my forehead and my first date was over.

When she had sent me the note, she was going steady with another boy. I didn't know until many, many years later that he had already asked her to marry him. Back then people made marriage plans earlier because of the war, and he was about ready to go into the service. After the prom she dated back and forth between the other guy and me for awhile, but somehow I ended up winning the prize.

When I was dating Rebecca and I would be going down the street on the way to her house, I would pass the house of Miss Jane Owen. She was a nice lady who wrote for the *Review Appeal*, and she would be sitting on her porch. She would say,

"Jimmy, are you going to see Rebecca tonight?" I would say, "Yes ma'am." She would look me over and say, "Well, have a nice time." People spent a lot of time on their porches or out in their yards, and they saw their neighbors almost every day. When something happened, everybody knew about it.

The first War Department telegram I ever saw delivered came by bicycle up Fifth Avenue, in front of the Methodist Church. We were living on the next block, and Mama had a blue star up for my brother David. Those people who had a blue star in their window would pray, "Please don't stop here. Please don't stop here." And he didn't stop at our house that day. He passed our house and turned up by Mrs. Josephine Wirt, who lived on the corner. He turned right on Margin Street to the corner of Margin and Cummins, and stopped at the Terry house. Everybody knew then that something had happened to Mack Terry. He had died on the Bataan Death March.

Those telegrams were delivered in different ways. Sometimes on a bicycle, sometimes on foot, and sometimes in an automobile. But no matter how it came, when that messenger showed up with a telegram, a soldier you knew was probably dead.

Not too long after that telegram came to the Terry's house, another telegram was brought to Franklin. It was springtime, and people were out in their yards. They saw the messenger coming, and they watched him come up to our house and stop. David had been on a bridge over the Minturno River in Italy. He had been stringing communications wire when the Germans shelled the bridge. He died on April 29, 1944, on the way to the field hospital. He was twenty-one years old.

My brother David

Mama took down the blue star she had put in the window for David and replaced it with a gold star, which signified his death. I think mothers probably suffered more than the soldiers during World War II. They would send their husbands and sons off to war, and then all they could do was wait and hope and pray. The anguish that Mama went through happened to mothers all over America, and they never received the recognition they should have gotten. I didn't find out that David was dead until I came home from school that day. I didn't go back to school except for graduation five days later. Mr. Thompson, my principal, called Mama and said I wasn't taking final exams.

I remembered how, when he was in high school, David had gotten a job promoting the movie, *The Lone Ranger*, when it was

coming to town. He had been furnished with a white horse, and he had some cap pistols and a cowboy hat. He rode up and down the street wearing a mask. I was so proud that he was my brother.

COMMITMENTS

Chapter Nine

At graduation there were only about twelve boys left in our class. Bobby Akin, who was probably my best friend during high school,  had gone into the service a few weeks earlier. Just before he left, he and Rebecca and I went over to the railroad track and he was shooting this .22 rifle he had. Bobby was a loner, but he was a nice guy and we really hit it off. After the graduation ceremony, out on the front steps of the high school, Mary Lavender, a friend of our family, came up and gave me a little white package with a red ribbon on it. She knew I would be going away to fight. She said,

Bobby Akin

"Jimmy, take this with you." I opened it, and it was a little New Testament with a metal shield on it. I put it in my pocket. It would be with me for the next two years of my life.

I kept working at Willow Plunge as a lifeguard, and that summer Rebecca was working there in the coffee shop. We had been going together for about a year, and one night when we were closing she was there waiting for me. We were going to walk home together. But we stayed around for awhile, up near the coffee shop, and we talked. Then before I realized what was happening, I said, "Will you marry me?" She didn't say anything at first, and I thought I had offended her. Then she said yes. But we decided we would wait until I came home from the war before we got married.

I didn't have an automobile, so a lot of times our dates were just me going over to Rebecca's home. A big night for us was to go to the movie in Franklin, or to catch the Interurban bus to Nashville and see a movie on Church Street, and maybe eat at Zunnini's Restaurant.

I had tried to join the Army Air Corps a little before my eighteenth birthday, but I found out during my physical examination that I was color-blind. I was told to go back home and wait because the Army would take anybody. I had friends who planned to go into the Air Force, and they kept talking about how they would be flying up above me while I was down on the ground. I got my orders to go into the army in the summer of 1944, not long after Rebecca and I decided to get married. The night before I left I spent some time at Rebecca's house, and we said our goodbyes. Leaving Rebecca was hard, but I had to accept it.

On the morning I went away, I told Mama goodbye before I left the house. She didn't show her emotions too much. She had known it was coming, and she accepted it the best way she could. She had just lost one son, and four months later she was sending off another one. After I left, she put a blue star in the window for me next to the gold star she'd put up for David.

I walked down Fifth Avenue and sat down on the wall in front of the Presbyterian Church—the same wall we had walked on top

of when we were children. I was one of 96 young men gathered there at Five Points who were going off to war. I knew nearly all of the other 95 and I thought, "Man, this is a sorry looking bunch. How can we win a war with a ragtag group like this?"

My attitude going into the service was that my country was being challenged. America had gotten into this war, and I wanted to be in the fight and make a contribution to my country. And I think everybody else was doing it for the same reason.

My name was called by Mr. Bob Jennings, who was in charge of the local draft board, and I hopped down off the rock fence and got on one of the buses. The buses took us to Fort Oglethorpe, Georgia, near Chattanooga. When we got there, we went into a big building with three desks. The middle desk was for the Army, and there were also desks for the Navy and the Coast Guard, but nobody was at the other desks. You couldn't get anything but the Army. They didn't need anything but foot soldiers. All those guys  who had been talking about flying above me in the Air Corps went into the infantry, too. We were all sworn in at Fort Oglethrope.

From there we went by rail to Camp McPherson, in Atlanta, Georgia, to get our uniforms, shots, and haircuts. They split up our group from Franklin when we got to Camp McPherson. It was done according to education. One group of boys who couldn't read or write were put together, and one or two guys who had gone to college were taken off somewhere else. Our street clothes were put in boxes and sent home. When you went into the service, you would give a lot of your clothes away to a brother or a friend, because you weren't going to need them. People didn't have too many clothes back then.

That train ride from Atlanta down through South Georgia was very, very hot. We pulled one of the windows open to get cool, but it was hotter outside than it was inside the train. Those steam engines would send little beads of hot water up out of the boiler, and they would go down your collar. We were wringing wet sitting there. It was that way all day long, and when the night came it didn't get a bit cooler. I kept thinking we will get there soon, but we just kept going and kept going.

We finally ended up a little bit over the Florida line at Camp Blanding, and there was nothing there but pine trees, sand, palmettos, and heat. That was where it all started. We walked across the sand, and I'd never been in sand before. We got to our hut, with 15 or 16 men assigned to each hut, and there was Sergeant LaCaze. He was sunburned, and he had a scar that looked like it went all the way across his face. He had gray hair and dark eyes that would look right through you. He was standing there staring at us when we came in, and then he said, "Nobody sits down." We were worn out. "Nobody sits down. Nobody lies down." We wondered what was wrong with him. He came around and gave everyone a little book, and he told us that breakfast was at 5:30, or something like that. "Know everything in this book by breakfast, but don't sit down."

The little book contained the General Orders. "I take charge of this post and all other government property in view," and a lot of other stuff, so I started learning it. We had a guy named Newman, and his bunk was right by the front door. Newman rolled his mattress out and lay down. Sergeant LaCaze grabbed that boy and pulled him up, and he yelled, "Get on the floor." He made him do pushups. Newman had little arms, and they were just quivering. I felt sorry for him, but he asked for it. Sergeant LaCaze left, and then he came back just before breakfast. Newman didn't know a single word of the General Orders.

Then Sergeant LaCaze said, "Walk to breakfast," but Newman and some others sprinted out the door to be first. When we came out of our hut, they were on the ground doing pushups in the sand,

81

and then they had to do all the dishes after breakfast. Sergeant LaCaze rode Newman's back, but Newman deserved it. We'd march and everybody would be in step but Newman. Sergeant LaCaze chewed him out, and I thought he was going to kill that guy. We finally began to feel sorry for Sergeant LaCaze because of this goof-off he had to put up with. He was causing us all kinds of trouble. But by the time we left he had finally become a soldier. I saw him shaking hands with Sergeant LaCaze. If it hadn't been for Sergeant LaCaze, Newman would've probably gotten himself killed as soon as he got into combat.

It was so hot at Camp Blanding that some nights you would move around on your cot just to try and find a dry spot. The whole mattress would be dripping with sweat. You would move around to find a little dry spot to get to sleep, and then it would get wet.

My background helped me. The hunting, the fishing, the athletics, the big family—all of it. The training wasn't a big problem for me. I already knew about weapons, but I had never fired one of those high-powered M1s or machine guns. They trained us with dynamite. They'd bundle up sticks of TNT and light them, and we had to hold them in our hands for a little bit before we threw them. They got us used to things like that, and to grenades and gas masks. I didn't have trouble with any of it. The highlight of my stay at Camp Blanding was a visit from my mother, my sisters Louise and Frances, and Rebecca. We were supposed to train for sixteen weeks, but after twelve weeks they told us to pack our stuff. We were leaving. "Boy," I wondered, "What is going on here?"

We went by train from Camp Blanding to Camp Kilmer, New Jersey. That's where we got our flannel uniforms, weapons, and all the rest of our gear. We got shots in both shoulders and both hips. Then the train took us to the harbor in New York. The size of the buildings was overwhelming. They put us on a ferry that had been used for automobiles, and then we came to a ship called the *USS Wakefield*. I looked up and up and up. It was taller than any of

the buildings back in Franklin. I had never seen anything that big, and I wondered how all that steel was going to float. There were lifeboats and rope ladders hanging all over it. It was a converted luxury liner, with four decks. Of course, I ended up on the lowest deck. The only thing between the water and me was a piece of steel. I think there must have been somewhere in the neighborhood of 10,000 foot soldiers on that ship. A couple of the guys who had been laughing at me for going in the infantry were on there, too— J.A. Hardison and Alva Jefferson.

At sea I didn't understand why the ship would go one way, then another. It would just zigzag. I thought, "Whoever is steering this ship is drunk." I had thought we would go right on over to England. But instead we kept zigzagging to keep German submarines from zeroing in on our ship.

I got seasick. I had never been that sick in my life, and I have never been that sick since. I was up in the top bunk, and guys were shooting craps down on the floor. When they heard old Gentry coming, they scattered like a bunch of quail. Finally I didn't have anything left to throw up. I would just heave all day and all night. I got so weak I could hardly move. Two guys finally climbed up and said, "Come on, you've got to eat." I said I couldn't eat, but they said I had to. They brought me down and held me up by my arms because I was too weak to stand on my own. They took me up to the galley. I ate some frankfurters, sauerkraut, beans, lemonade, and a piece of bread. It was pretty good, but then this guy right across from me went "Bluhe," and threw up in his tray. I threw up too, but I finally got to where I could eat a little bit.

We landed at Liverpool after thirteen days at sea. I was up on the top deck, and I could see Liverpool out below me in what was left of the daylight. A little after midnight, they said to get our stuff and get ready. We got all our equipment and then got in line

and took hold of the belt of the man in front. I had his belt and somebody behind me had my belt. Then they turned the lights out, and that was about the last time I saw electric lights at night for six months.

Liverpool was blacked out, and the ship was blacked out. If the Germans had any spies, they wouldn't have been able to tell how many of us there were or what kind of soldiers we were. I could tell when we got on the gangplank, because it swayed a little bit. When we got to the train, an officer had a little penlight to get us in our seats. There were black shades pulled down when the train left. When we were allowed to pull up the shades, it was early in the morning. British children would run to the railroad and wave. They wanted us to throw them some candy.

The train brought us to South Hampton, and we got on an LST, a big landing craft where the front would drop down into a ramp. There were a couple of half-tracks on there with us. I got up in one of the half-tracks and went to sleep. Sometime during the night we started out across the English Channel. I was dreaming I was sick, and then I woke up and found out I really was sick, but I got over that pretty quickly. It didn't take us long to get across the English Channel.

THE WORLD OF WAR

Chapter Ten

We landed at Le Havre. D-Day had happened a few months earlier, but there was still lots of debris around. We got within about thirty feet of the beach, and then we waded to shore. It was really cold, and it was beginning to snow. Just after I got to the beach, I heard somebody call out my name. It was Beverly Chadwell. I couldn't believe I was seeing somebody from home. I must have been the last person from Williamson County who saw him alive. Beverly was killed not too many weeks after that as our forces were crossing the Rhine.

Then they loaded us into boxcars. Man, it was cold. They took us a little way, and then they put us in trucks. The trucks took us a little farther, and then we got out and went into this bombed-out building. We were still cold, but it kept us out of the snow. Finally, a jeep came up and my name was called along with another guy. They said, "Get in the jeep," and there we went.

We got to a little French village called Pettincourt that was about 95 percent destroyed. It was really snowing heavily, and we could hear the big guns in the distance. They sounded like thunder. We found a building that only had the windows blown out, and we went into a room upstairs and put a blanket over the window. We found a little stove about three feet tall, and we started burning anything we could find. We burned the banister and the hand-rails from the steps, but there was no furniture left anywhere. So we went out into some other buildings and  found something else to burn. There were seven of us in there, and we lay around the stove talking and trying to keep warm.

One of the guys was named Michael, and he was from Chicago. I hadn't seen too many real live, up close Yankees before. He was a great big guy, and he was older than the rest of us. We were about 19 years old and clean-shaven, but he had a beard and he smoked a cigar. Michael would talk, gosh, he would talk, and the more he talked about how tough he was, the more I thought the German army didn't have a chance. Michael was on our side, and it sounded like he could whip them all by himself.

About 11 o'clock that night a runner came up from the command post and told us to fall out and draw ammunition. We knew we were getting close to the fighting. We went down and got our two bandoleers of bullets, and then we got a couple of hand grenades and went back upstairs to wait. Michael was still talking, but he was a little bit subdued by that point. Everything was getting quieter all the time, and then the same runner came back, and our captain said, "Fall out." We all went down the stairs and out into the snow, and there were no lights anywhere. All Michael's talking had made us feel confident, but we lost our confidence pretty soon.

We got into the back of a truck, and when they pulled down the tarp, we couldn't see anything. Nobody was talking—you could just hear people breathing. The truck started easing forward, and I remember being more scared than I'd ever been. I didn't know where I was, and I didn't know where I was going. I didn't know if I was going to be alive five minutes later. I prayed silently, "God, please take care of me," over and over, and I'm sure the others did, too. All of a sudden we all heard Michael praying out loud. He was saying the same thing I was praying. Then we knew he was just like the rest of us. The only place to go was to the Lord in prayer, but Michael didn't end up making it through the war.

Finally, they let us out. They had taken us up into the mountains to relieve the 45th Division. Another soldier and I relieved a guy who had a one-man foxhole, so we had to enlarge the hole to fit the two of us. We had to dig in before dawn so we wouldn't be above ground when it got light.

Those first few nights we nearly froze to death. We spent most of the time trying to keep our fingers and our feet from getting frostbite. But if I had grown up in a heated house it would've been even worse, so it was probably good that I'd suffered a little bit on those winter nights back in Williamson County. We would take our boots off and rub each other's feet just as hard as we could to keep the circulation going. We stayed in our foxhole during the day. The only time we would come out was at night. The only thing that could kill you at night was artillery.

It didn't take very long to tell the difference between our artillery going out from the German artillery coming in. The sounds were different. The rest of our squad was spread out around us in foxholes. There was a pretty good hole in the middle of our position, so at night a soldier from each of the other holes would crawl over there and start digging to make it bigger. We dug until it was about six feet by eight feet. You couldn't stand up in it, but at least you could crawl around and sit up. From then on we all stayed in the big foxhole.

My squad was part of E Company of the 232nd Infantry Regiment. We had John Farley, who was from Bay City, Michigan. He was small and baby-faced, but he was smart and tough and he knew how to take care of himself. Ernest Wayka was a Menominee Indian from Neopit, Wisconsin. He was older than the rest of us. He was a good solider, and when he talked, it almost sounded like a grunt. Carl Hart was from Hale, Missouri. He was a short, stocky guy. He was very reliable, and I really trusted him. Ira Whaley was a big, strong, easy-going guy from Alabama. We could count on Ira to do whatever needed to be done. James Briggs was a dark-haired guy from New Castle, Indiana. He was sort of independent, but he could always be counted on when there was trouble. My best friend in the squad was Charlie Theisen from Long Island, New York. He was a solid soldier with a great sense of humor.

When German shells hit the trees, we called it "tree burst." Big limbs, branches, and parts of trunks would come crashing down. Ernest Wayka was good with a hatchet, and he trimmed those logs up and we would put them over our foxhole. So we had a hole with logs over it, and we covered it with a new material I had never heard of before. It was called gas cape, or plastic. We rolled it out on top of the logs, and covered it with dirt and pine needles to keep the melting snow from dripping down on us or the rain from getting in. We also put pine needles five or six inches deep inside the foxhole, and then we would get inside and try to use our body heat to stay warm. That's how we survived the cold and the artillery.

You didn't relieve yourself in the daytime. It might have been your last trip. You relieved yourself just before dawn or right after dark. You'd go out on the side of the mountain, and if you did a number two, you would have to put up a little stick that we called a flag to mark where you'd gone. We stayed there about three weeks. When we left there were flags all over the side of that hill.

The nights were interesting. You could hear everything. If a bird flew or something moved, it would scare you. You would hear a wild boar, and you thought it might be an enemy patrol. Sometimes somebody got scared, and they would start shooting in the dark. The company commander would yell, "Cut that out." You didn't want to give your position away. If you heard something suspicious, you got the platoon leader to call for "night light." The artillery would fire a shell that would explode and light up the whole area. Sometimes they would do that, and there would just be a deer walking around. So you didn't light any kind of fire, you didn't strike a match, and you didn't even wear a watch with a radium dial. The Germans could see them at night. Very few soldiers had watches, just the platoon leaders.

Every night we would hear "Bed Check Charlie," the German observation plane, come over. We could tell the sound of his plane from ours. He would go back and forth all night long. He was looking for light, so when he got back the Germans could figure out exactly where our lines were. Then their artillery could zero in on us. We would sit real quiet, and we could hear the German trucks and tanks moving across the way. I can hear them right now.

One night a guy named Raymond Ratzel and I were called back to pull guard duty at the command post. It was about one in the morning, and the two of us were in a hole. Raymond was killing time, and he pulled the pin out of his hand grenade. He dropped it in the bottom of our foxhole into the mud and he couldn't find it. A hand grenade will not detonate until a little lever is released. As long as he held that lever down, it would not explode. We couldn't find the pin in the mud. I threatened to make Raymond stay outside for the rest of the night. But I ended up taking one of his bootlaces, and I tied the lever down as tight as I could and rolled the grenade away from our foxhole. I never did find out what happened to that grenade because we went back to our unit the next day.

Another time it was Carl Hart's time to be on guard duty, and we said, "Carl, get on out there." He said, "Let me fix me a hot cup of coffee." He got it too hot, and when he got out there, he put his cup down on a log. Then he heard one of their shells coming in, and he came diving in on top of us. That shell hit, everything finally settled down, and Carl crawled back out. We could hear him out there mumbling, "They got my coffee." A piece of shrapnel went through that coffee cup without turning it over, and drained out every drop. Another piece went through the box he had been sitting on.

The worst thing we had to deal with was shrapnel. We didn't have Germans trying to slip across on us. We'd have patrols go out to get information, and if they had missed the password for the day they would whistle, "The camels are coming." We didn't have too many shots coming over on us. We were dug in, and we were relativity safe unless we got a direct hit, which would have gotten us all. The cold was just as big an enemy as the German artillery.

I was 19 years old, I had left the streets of Franklin just a few months earlier, and there I was in a hole in the ground in France. I would think of back home and my family all the time. I knew I was truly in love. Rebecca would write each day, and I would write when I could. Everybody wanted to go home, but you knew you weren't going to go home. You had to accept being where you were. You just resigned yourself to the fact that you were there. It was just get through this day. Get through this hour. Get through this moment. Keep going until this is over with. But for some reason I felt confident that I was going to get back home.

Mr. Thompson had let Rebecca come back to high school to qualify as a typist. She got a job working at the ration board in Franklin. She would see the German POWs getting out of the trucks from Camp Campbell. The local farmers would pick them up to work in the fields. They didn't need guards. If one of them ran away, where would he go?

One day they came up and said we were going to get us a little R&R, rest and relaxation. They'd only let two or three of us go at a time. My turn came, and I went back through the mountains to a little farmhouse that had a chicken house right beside it. It took about 40 minutes to get back there. Between the farmhouse and the chicken house there were these big barrels of hot water. So I took off the top part of my clothes, and bathed the upper part of my body, and then I put my clothes back on fast. Gosh, it was cold. Then I took off my pants and bathed my bottom half and then put them back on right quick, too. So that was what they called rest and relaxation. It was the first time I'd gotten to clean up since I left Camp Kilmer, New Jersey. I wouldn't have another bath until the war was over.

We didn't have a toothbrush or toothpaste. Mama had told me how people had cleaned their teeth when she was a girl. They would break off a wild cherry twig and chew the last half-inch until it was soft with little bristles. So that's what I did, and some guys in my platoon were puzzled by my homemade toothbrush. She had also told me to use soda and salt to clean my teeth, and later on I would get soda and salt from houses we'd pass. We shaved as often as we could. We heated water in canteen cups and used safety razors. Almost everyone stayed clean-shaven, even through shaving with cold water hurt. I didn't worry about how I smelled, because everybody else smelled the same way.

We ate K-rations all the time. We had three separate meals: one was green and white camouflage, one was blue and white camouflage, and the other one was brown and white camouflage. We carried them in the hoods of our combat jackets when we were moving. The cans were different, but all of them basically had the same things inside. Green and white was breakfast. There would be chopped eggs and ham. There were some little crackers I called dog biscuits, and there were also three Chelsea cigarettes, a stick of chewing gum, and a little roll of toilet paper. That was it. Then at lunch the can was blue and white. You had things like processed American cheese, three crackers, three more cigarettes, and toilet paper. I didn't smoke, so I gave my cigarettes away or I sold them. The other guys were glad to see me get my cigarettes. Then at supper we had the brown and white can. There was potted meat of some sort, three crackers, and maybe a fig bar along with powdered instant coffee, which was a new thing.

INTO GERMANY

Chapter Eleven

We stayed right in the same place till the weather began to change. The German tanks and trucks started to retreat, and we were on our way. One night loud speakers were brought up and put in the trees where we were. The Germans were told that if they gave up and surrendered, they would get food, cigarettes, and some other things. They were also told that if they didn't surrender by such and such time, they were going to experience the biggest bombardment in the history of World War II. I remember seeing two Germans finally come across before the bombardment and ask for their cigarettes. It was a good thing for them that they did. That night the shelling started at 6 o'clock. The ground vibrated. We fired mortars, the big guns behind us fired off the big shells, and the planes dropped bombs. We just wrecked that place. There were trees down everywhere, and after a while we moved forward. We knew where our minefields were, and our folks had done a good job of cleaning out their mines, because we got safely over to their side. The Germans had moved out.

We were going along a path through the woods, and there was a German shoe with a foot still in it—just like someone had taken a knife and cut it off. It had probably happened during the bombardment. The Germans had notched some trees beside the road. They had tied dynamite on the back-sides of the trees, and they would set if off with batteries. The trees would all blow at once and fall across the road. Not even tanks could get through, but we found a way to keep moving.

EXPLOSIVES

Our rations were supposed to be sent·up on mules, but they didn't come. Finally Sergeant Jacobe took three or four guys and went back and found the mules grazing on the mountain side. The men leading them had said there were too many mines and booby traps and Germans, and they wouldn't come up any closer.

We ate, and then we kept going up and up that mountain. It was a whole lot worse than Roper's Knob back home. General Linden saw me filling my canteen from a small mountain stream. He yelled at me, "You are going to have a stomach ache," and he never stopped. I went ahead and drank the water, and I never got a stomach ache. It was after dark when we finally got close to a village. We could see the buildings down below us, along with some German trucks and vehicles. The company commander said we were going to wait till morning to attack. He said the Germans didn't know we were up there. We had moved faster than they thought we would.

We couldn't dig in because the ground was frozen, so we piled on top of one another to try to stay as warm as we could. I was in a pile of 15 or 20 men. The bottom man was cold from the ground, but warm on top. The man on top was cold on the top side of his body, but warm on the bottom side. The one in the middle was in good shape. We were like a bunch of worms moving around all night trying to get a good place. We'd try to work one guy out and get where he was. We made it through the night that way.

Some of the others slept in groups of three, leaning against each other. Each man had his arms on his knees and leaned forward. They tried to stay warm that way. They had to sleep sitting up. The ground was frozen, and it was too cold to lie down. One of our guys accidentally fired his weapon while he was leaning on it that night, and it killed him. That must have alerted the Germans that we were close, and during the night they moved out.

It took us awhile to get down to the village. There was just a church and a few little buildings, and they were all torn up. The company commander said we were going to spend the night in the church. Half of the church roof was gone, and one of the walls was mostly missing. We tried to sleep on pews in that church and we nearly froze to death. Somebody finally found a furnace behind the pulpit and built a fire in it. Only 20 or 30 men could get close enough to stay warm, but we made it through that night.

By the next morning our tanks had come up, and we were told to get on the tanks. I thought, "Man, this is good news." We had been walking the whole time. So we got on those tanks and took off. There was only one problem—tanks draw fire. The Germans didn't see an individual nearly as soon as they saw a big, noisy tank, and when their observation planes found one, they started firing. We had to jump off, and I never got on another tank after that.

The shells would hit close enough to ring your ears. I couldn't believe how loud those explosions were. What I think was a 155 Howitzer went off to my right, and I couldn't hear for the rest of that day. It really shook me up. I lost some of the hearing in my right ear, but it wasn't from shells coming in—it was from the ones going out. We were moving up through some artillery fire to take a new position. They would move you out, then move you over, and then put you back into the line wherever they needed help.

We didn't meet a lot of opposition at first. While we were moving, we found an abandoned German dugout. It had plank floors, bunks, and a stove. It was really nice. Finally we got to the Siegfried line. There were pillboxes and what were called tiger teeth, which were concrete structures built to keep the tanks from coming through. We reached a little village, and we could see the Germans in the distance across a field. One of our tanks came up behind the farm-house where we were positioned, and the Germans opened up on us.

They shelled us pretty heavily behind the farmhouse and at the edge of the woods. I was scared of the artillery. You couldn't see it coming. All of a sudden it would come in and explode and blow everything apart. The Germans used the same methods all the artillery men used. The first round was usually off target, but the shots that followed would be closer and closer to the target. So when they fired on us, we would run and get in the hole made by that first round.

That night a shell exploded in front of us, and the next one went behind us. We had learned what to do when that happened— you had better get out of there. So a couple of other guys and I ran up and jumped in the first hole, and sure enough the third shell exploded right where we had been. It destroyed the whole area. I don't know how many other guys got hurt. We just stayed in that hole for the rest of the night.

Later on a German patrol came right up to the hole where we were. We could see their silhouettes. We didn't open fire on them because we didn't want them to know where we were. They turned around pretty soon and went back. By the next morning we were really pinned down. We couldn't do anything, but our dive-bombers and our artillery either destroyed the people in the pill-boxes or made them fall back. Then we moved on across the Siegfried Line without much problem. The road was littered with burning vehicles, and there were a lot of dead horses. We were in the Alsace Lorraine district of France, which was  south of the main fighting in the Battle of the Bulge. The Germans had attacked the area where I happened to be in order to draw our troops to the south.

We continued to advance, and sometime in March, after the snow had melted, we were going up a hillside toward a village on a hill. Somebody shot a German lookout who was hiding in a tree. He was hit in the arm, and the hole looked as big as a baseball. It took out a big piece of his upper arm. He was screaming like crazy, and we took him to a house where the medics gave him enough morphine to knock him out. We moved on through the little village, and then later we were forced back. We came back to the same house, and that guy was still lying on the floor. Some other troops had come up behind us and some other medic had given him more morphine. I don't know whether the poor guy lived or not.

We finally got to the Rhine River and crossed at Worms. Now we were in Germany, and we had a different feeling. When we were fighting in France we knew the war was a long way from being over, but when we got to Germany it was like we were in the fourth quarter of a football game, and we wanted to make sure we won that last quarter. After we got across the Rhine, they put us into a forced march. We moved as fast as we could until we met opposition. As long as we didn't meet opposition, we kept going.

We would walk all day, staying five yards apart. The reason we walked five yards apart was so one shell couldn't kill too many people. There was no stopping for anybody. If you needed to relieve yourself, you ran as fast as you could up through the column, you relieved yourself, and you hoped you could get back to your spot. You ate while you walked. Sometimes we didn't have anything to eat.

If we were lucky a tank would come by, and they always had extra K-rations. They would throw down a crate of K-rations, and when it hit the ground, the crate would break open and we would eat.

Occasionally we would find a house along the road, and if there was no combat going on right then, we would go in the house and go down and look in the cellar for food. Sometimes we might find glass jugs full of apples, pears, peaches, and things like that. We would carry our spoons down in our boots, and we would walk along eating whatever we'd gotten. Somebody might holler, "I've got some peaches," and I'd say, "Well, I'll swap you some pears." That is how we supplemented our diets.

So once we got into Germany we'd go all day, and when night came we'd just keep going. We didn't stop. You would get so tired that you might go to sleep while you were walking. You'd just fall asleep and then you'd hit the ground, and that woke you up. Then you got back up and kept walking. I can only remember falling asleep while I was walking one time, and that was before dawn on the morning of April 3, 1945. That morning we could hear thunder and see flashes in the sky. We thought that we were walking into a terrible thunderstorm, but it wasn't a thunderstorm.

WÜRZBURG

Chapter Twelve

The British Air Force was bombing Würzburg, Germany with incendiary bombs that night, and then early in the morning the American Air Force came in and continued the bombing. We were about seventy miles east of the Rhine, and we saw the glow and the flashes from where the city was burning and exploding. Close to dawn the bombing stopped. Then the artillery behind us started firing into the city. They just destroyed Würzburg.

We were trying to get across the Main River before dawn. If we hadn't gotten across before dawn, we would have been easy targets out in that river. Although most of the buildings were de-molished, the walls were still standing, and the Germans could've done a lot of damage from behind that sort of cover. We got there right at dawn and found our engineers building a bridge across the water. I learned that we were able to get across without any casualties, because the Germans thought we were German soldiers retreating.

Once we got across to Würzburg, there was a wide cobble-stone street with the river on one side and buildings and walls on the other side. When you kept your back up against the walls, they couldn't get a shot at you. While we were working our way along those walls, I looked back across the river at this huge old fortress on a hill, and I saw the words "Heil, Hitler" painted in letters eight feet high. Later that same day I looked back, and some GI had climbed up and painted "42nd Rainbow Division" over "Heil, Hitler".

It was still early in the morning, and while I was standing there, a door just to my left opened. I looked over and this handsome, elderly gentleman was coming out. He had on civilian clothes and a dark suit. As soon as he came out of the door, he said in English, "Thank God you Americans are here." He went to the right, in the direction we were going, and he dis-appeared. A little later we moved up, and I saw him lying dead in the street. I don't know who shot him.

We were able to go through several blocks of ruins before we came to a bombed-out building. We climbed through some windows, and it was full of rubble. Our objective was right across the street—Old University and Neubau Church. The church was left standing out of respect for religion, and Germans soldiers were still inside the church. We had to get them out. They had us pretty well pinned down, and Sergeant Randy McDavid, from South Carolina, was killed by Germans who were firing from that church. I was only ten feet away from him when it happened. We were all looking out to see where the firing was coming from, and he was shot right between the eyes.

We were also receiving fire from what was left of a building off to our right. One of their soldiers was behind a big column, and we couldn't get a clear shot at him. So we started firing at the rubble beside him, and one of the ricochets finally hit him. He fell out from behind that column and died in the street. Then somebody said, "Hey, they are going to get us if we don't move." So we all got up and ran across the street just like gangbusters, and we ran right into the church.

Just about the first thing we saw was ten or twelve caskets. There probably hadn't been time to have the funerals yet. The German soldiers had been up in the church tower, but they had come down and gone into the back of the church. When they realized we were in the building, they started going out the windows in the back. Our troops picked them up outside. So we were able to clear them out, but by that time it was nearly dark. It had taken us all day and we had only gone several blocks. We didn't sleep that night either. We were on guard duty. All night long we could hear footsteps in the dark. There was a little light from some of the buildings that were still burning, and we could see movement in the shadows. It was spooky. There were German soldiers all around us.

The city of Würzburg was the toughest fighting my company ran into. The next day came, and we spent a lot of time running from building to building. There was nothing but rubble, and we tried to take our positions in places where we thought we wouldn't be shot. For five or six blocks we darted from one spot to another, and by the afternoon we had reached a grassy, shaded park.

There were bombed-out buildings all around us, and we didn't realize that the Germans were everywhere. They had pulled back into the buildings around that park. The sun had come out, and it had gotten warm. We hadn't slept in two days and two nights. We were exhausted. I nodded off while I was lying on the ground, just before we were moved a little farther into the park.

Then all of a sudden the Germans let us have it. We were taking machine gun fire from every direction. At first we thought the fire was only coming from the front, but they were also on both sides of us. I found a big tree, and I thought if I hid behind that tree, they couldn't get me. Then a bullet went by, and it sounded like someone had taken a rubber band and popped a piece of paper with it. Bullets started popping and tree branches were falling all around, and some guys were hit just to my right.

Somebody behind me hollered, "They're after you!" I yelled back, "I know it." I would move around the tree, but I was still an  open target. Then a shot ricocheted off the tree and hit my helmet. It cut a groove right through the steel part. It was like I had been hit with a hammer. It knocked the day-lights out of me. I knew what had happened. I just went down and lay there. The next thing I knew, two guys were pulling me away by my feet. One of them said, "Hey, he's alive!" That was the closest I ever got to being killed. I had been less than an inch from being dead. At the time it didn't bother me too much, but it scared me later on.

We really counted on our mortars, but as we were trying to advance through the park, we ran out of mortar shells. Charlie Theisen and I volunteered to go back for what we needed. We were under fire most of the way going and coming. I would run as fast as I could into the ruins of a building. Then I'd try to catch my breath and run over to a building across the street. I'd try not to come out the same place I'd gone in. There were bullets zipping by Charlie and me the whole way, but we made it back, got the shells, and then we went through the whole thing all over again. It was about three blocks from our position to the rear, but it seemed like three miles. Both Charlie and I were awarded Bronze stars for that later on. I was also given a second Bronze Star, but I never knew what it was for. They must have had so many, that they had to give them to somebody. Being awarded the Bronze Star was an honor, but I was just as proud of the Combat Infantry Badge that was issued to everyone who served in combat.

We finally got through the park, and night was coming. We made it to some houses that were next to the park. Vehicles and troops were coming across the river and pouring into the city. We were exhausted, and the decision was made to let us sleep that night. We slept under the ledge of the upstairs floor of a house that had burned. There was some coal under the ledge, and I just went to sleep on the coal.

The next morning I heard somebody call out my name. There was a man in a fancy uniform coming up the street, and we went out and captured him. We thought we had captured somebody important. He had on a satin uniform with those things on the shoulders. We found out later we'd captured a streetcar conductor. He should have stayed home that day.

A little later on I heard my name called again, but this time it was for mail call. Getting mail was the only thing we had to look forward to during the war. When you heard your name called out, that meant that you had mail. So this guy was standing on the seat of a jeep and he called my name six times. And then he called it out again for a package. I was so happy. So I got my letters and my package, and I went off and sat down.

107

We had a guy in our squad named Jack, and he never got any mail. So I sat down and when I was opening my first letter, Jack, who was sitting about four feet from me said, "Hey Gentry, do you mind if I read one of your letters?" And I said, "No, Jack, you take three of them. We'll read them and swap." We did that from then on whenever I got mail. Inside the package was Eagle Brand milk, Hershey chocolate syrup, and sugar wafers, and it was all wrapped up in a wool vest that Rebecca had made. We'd made a fire with the coal we found, and eating that food from home beside the fire was the best meal I'd tasted in my whole life.

We left the downtown area later that morning, and we moved out into a residential area. We got to where the street we were on dead-ended into another street, and I saw a German soldier running away. I notified the platoon, and we went over to try and see where he'd gone. We passed two or three houses that looked abandoned. It was a real cold morning, and we came to a house that had fogged-up windows and a little steam coming out from around the cracks. We knew there was heat in that house, and we thought the guy I'd seen running away must have been a lookout who'd gone back to warn his buddies.

So some of our squad went to the front of the house, and some went around to the back. I got on the side of the house, next to a hedge that was two or three feet high. We had them trapped. I could hear them inside yelling, "Nich Schiesen! Nich Schiesen!" which meant, "Don't shoot!"

But one of their guys decided he wasn't going to give up. He started easing out of a coal chute right next to where I was standing. I heard a noise, and I looked down and saw the glass door to the chute being raised. He pushed out his rifle, and then he pushed out a hand grenade that we called a potato masher. Then I saw his black helmet. I wasn't nervous—I knew I had him. He crawled out on his hands and knees, and just as he started to stand up, I pushed the safety off my rifle. He heard the click and looked up. He knew he didn't have a chance. If he had resisted I would have shot him right there, but he surrendered and I took him prisoner. The other 20 or 30 of them came out of the house with their hands on their heads, and we sent them off down to the foot of the hill.

Before we left Würzburg we went back to the park, and there were 300 or 400 POWs standing in three lines with their hands on their heads. Some of our officers were going up and down the line, taking their watches and whatever else they could find. I was at the end of one of the lines. One of the prisoners caught my eye. I went over to him and he motioned to his pocket. He wanted me to take the watch out of his pocket. I guess he didn't want the officers to have it. I pulled it out, and he nodded okay, take it. So I took it and later on I sent it home to my brother William.

SURGING FORWARD

Chapter Thirteen

From Würzburg we went toward a small village called Arnstein. We moved up to a hill, and we could see that the road we were on passed a farmhouse and went on through an open field. Then the road reached a bridge that went across a deep creek. On the other side of the creek there was a high bank. We went on down the road to the farmhouse, and we saw all these German civilians coming out of Arnstein.

When we would move forward, civilians would usually move back away from us. But this time they were coming our way. We should have known something was wrong. They were pushing buggies, bicycles, and wagons and they were carrying babies. Just as we started across the field in front of the bridge, the Germans opened up on us from the high bank on the other side of the creek. They had all their guns dug in on that side, and everybody hit the ground. The open field had alfalfa growing in it, and we got down in the alfalfa. I was near the house, so I crawled back and hid behind it. We set up our mortars behind the house.

They couldn't get to us with their panzerfaust, which was the name for a German bazooka. We were shooting mortars over the house, but then one of our guys got hit about thirty yards out in front of the house, and he couldn't move. He hollered back, "I'm hit," and we told him to put sulfur on his wound. You were supposed to put sulfur tablets on your wounds, and you were also supposed to drink a lot of water, but he didn't have any water, so we got some canteens. I'm right-handed, so I got on one side of a window facing the enemy, and a left-handed guy got on the other side, and we threw canteens through the window. And the whole time we were throwing canteens, the bullets were coming at us  through the windows. Wood and plaster was flying off the wall behind us, but we finally got a canteen close enough so he could get some water.

After awhile we heard a big roar coming up behind us. It was one of our TDs, a tank destroyer. It was bigger than a tank. It had an open turret and a 90mm gun that could knock out tanks. It started shooting into the top of the embankment above the creek, and it really worked over those guys who had been shooting at us. After that things quieted down, and we went up and crossed the bridge, but we lost one guy who was hit and fell in the creek.

We had gone across the bridge and we were moving down the road when I heard somebody hollering. It was a Mexican medic with us, and he couldn't speak English very well. He had been walking on top of the bank above the road. I didn't know what he was hollering, but he was pointing at the ground. We went up there, and the ground was loose and it was moving. One of the shells from our TD had hit the bank, and it had covered up the Germans who were down in the hole with their machine guns.

I got down on my hands and knees and started digging. I dug down and found a black helmet, and cleared out the dirt around it. I got my hands underneath the front of the helmet and there was this face breathing into one of my hands. We were digging the dirt out from around his head, and some civilians came along. We got them up there with shovels and pointed to where we'd started uncovering some other guys who were buried. They started covering them back up. We shouted, "Get them out! We want them

out!" They dug down and dug down and finally they got them out. They pulled up the guy I'd found, but he collapsed and rolled down the bank. He had been hit right in the base of his neck, and he died right there. That fight by the creek was our last big skirmish.

We were on our way toward Schweinfurt, Germany, where there was an important ball-bearing plant. We moved around a hill to the north of the city, and I saw the bombers coming in. I saw a big smokestack shake and then collapse. Buildings were blowing up all over the place. We were on one of the roads coming out of

the city, and after a while, after we finally quit bombing, there were a bunch of retreating German soldiers coming toward us. We were up on the hill waiting for them. As soon as they saw us, they put their hands up. They had two American pilots who had been their prisoners, and we got them both. Then we turned around and went back to the south.

Just before dark, when we were on our way from Schweinfurt to Nuremburg, we began to get very thirsty. We could still see a little bit and there was a barn, and right outside the barn was a pump. We thought, oh boy, now we can get some water, so we went over and got our canteens out. Somebody started pumping away, and all of a sudden there was this awful smell. What came out was urine from the cattle. They would wash off the floor of the barn, and it would all run down into a tank underneath. Then they would pump it out into wooden wagons, and they would spray it back on their field. We didn't do much drinking there.

From there we moved on toward Buchdorf, picking up a lot of prisoners along the way. Just before we went into Buchdorf we were on the side of the hill above a little village. A jeep came up with the forward observer for the 232nd field artillery, who would get on his radio and direct artillery fire. He was a good guy. His jeep was coming up the road, and all of a sudden there was a big explosion. I saw that jeep go eight or ten feet up in the air, and he was six or eight feet above the jeep. He was a big man over 200 pounds. The jeep driver had run over a mine. It killed the forward observer, but the driver survived.

We started down into the village, and there was a German lady out in front of the very first house we reached. She was standing out there offering us pieces of pie. I thought about how it could be poison, but I went ahead and tried some anyway. It was good. It tasted like sweet potato pie. We went into another house a little farther on, and we found a big basket full of eggs. The stove was hot, and I thought, "Man, looky here." We couldn't find any skillets, so we just started breaking eggs and cooking them on top of the stove. But we didn't have time to stand around and eat. We were called outside, and we had to scoop up those hot eggs and eat them on the run. They burned our hands, but they sure tasted good.

It was still early in the morning, and the German infantry was dug in on the east side of a small village near Buchdorf. About 100 yards beyond the same village, the road made a sharp turn to the right. The Germans were waiting to ambush us in the woods in the curve of the little road. Our first platoon surprised them by attacking from our right and the Germans were forced out of the woods. Then they tried to move across some open ground to more woods on our left. One of them was hit, and some others raised their hands. When we reached the wounded enemy soldier, he had a wound in his left buttock that was big enough to hold a good-sized grapefruit.

We were moving toward the end of the village, and everything seemed okay, but when we got close to another farmhouse, our company commander, Lieutenant John Lindberg, was hit in the

chest by a burst of machine gun fire and he died outright. Lieutenant Lindberg was from Minnesota, and he had a wife and two children at home. He was a very good officer. He was a lanky, good-natured guy, and we respected him.

Not too long after that we were moving in the darkness, and we came to another village. We couldn't see anything. We would move our hands along the walls of the buildings, and we finally decided we would just stop and spend the night. We didn't have a tent or a sleeping bag—we just slept anywhere we could. Three of us had gotten to be pretty close, Charlie Theisen, an Indian named Yazzi, and I. We were at the corner of a building, and it was my turn to sit down and rest.

All of a sudden I heard Charlie say, "Get up, get up." He was kicking me. He said, "Somebody's coming", and while I was getting up, I heard one of our guys say, "Halt." I could tell it was the Germans because they had hobnail boots, and hobnail boots sounded different from our boots. They halted and put their weapons down, and then they were taken away in the dark. The next morning we saw the weapons they had surrendered. There were machine guns and panzerfaust, and all sorts of equipment on the road. There must have  been 50 to 75 soldiers who had surrendered the night before. The Germans were in full retreat. They were moving back so fast that it was hard for us to keep up with them.

From Buchdorf we went south to the Danube River. It helped that I had grown up on the Harpeth. Some guy said, "Does anybody know how to paddle a boat?" I said I could. Most of the guys didn't know anything about paddling. We were going to cross the Danube on rafts, and some officer made a mistake that could've gotten some of our men killed. We were all wearing what we called ammo capes, which contained six mortar shells that weighed three pounds each. The weight of the shells along with our weapons would have made anybody who went into the water drown if a raft had turned over. They should've had us take them off and then put them back on when we got across the river. The river was pretty swift. We started out pretty far upstream and ended up pretty far downstream. It was really dangerous and dumb, but we made it across.

From there we headed on toward Munich. The Germans were out of equipment, materials, and shells. We could shell the daylights out of them. Every time there was a fight, they lost. They were down, and they were really getting kicked.

Horror and Prayer

Chapter Fourteen

A few days later, on April 29, 1945, at about five o'clock in the morning, my company, E Company, 232nd Infantry Regiment, 2nd Battalion, 42nd Infantry Division, ran across Dachau Concentration Camp. We didn't know anything about Dachau—we thought we were going to Munich. Around 11 o'clock that morning we arrived at a slope that led down to a wall that was about 20 feet high. Whatever was on the other side of that wall smelled awful. We thought it might have been some kind of gas that the Germans were using. We were at the northwest corner of this wall, near some open gates that trains would come through. There were boxcars partly outside the gate, and we saw some more inside.

Some of the other guys and I went to the boxcars. We saw hundreds of dead bodies. They were in uniforms, but they weren't soldiers. The uniforms had black and white stripes. The biggest parts of their bodies were the heads. The eyes were rolled back and sunken in. They had ashen white skin, legs and arms the size of broomsticks, and you could see every rib in their bodies. Some had spilled out onto the tracks, some were still in the boxcars, and some were half in and half out. They were all dead.

I remember saying, "Who are these people?" Someone said, "They're Jews." I didn't understand. The only Jewish people I knew were a couple of families in Franklin. Mr. Martin Tohrner, the man who bought pelts from my brother and me, was Jewish and he was one of my best friends. So I said, "Why Jews?"

We went into the camp. There were dead people in the streets. There were warehouses, which were the barracks of the SS troops, Germany's elite soldiers. We went from

building to building, securing each one we came to. I was in one of the buildings, and we came to a locked door. We knocked out a big pane of opaque glass and reached in and opened the door. It was the Commandant's office. There was a closet, and I found a bunch of uniforms hanging in there. I also found a .25 caliber automatic pistol in a holster, and I took it with me.

We had come through the railroad gate, and some other troops had come in the front gate. About the time we linked up with them

I saw a barbed wire fence inside the wall, a moat with water, and then another wall with barbed wire on top of it. I thought, "What in the world have they got inside this wall?" We went through the main gate of the compound, and then I saw all these prisoners staring out through the barbed wire at us. It was a sea of faces. 200, 300, 1,000—I don't know how many there were. There were probably 30 or 40 of us standing there. Those people were looking out at us, and we were looking in at them.

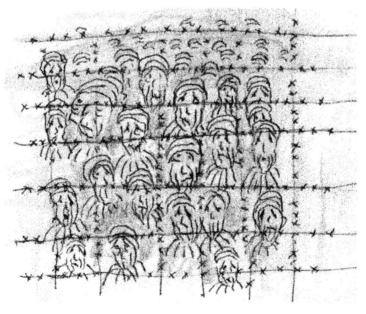

When we went in, they started grabbing our arms and legs, they kissed our legs, and they kissed our boots. The smell was awful. Somebody said, "Don't let them kiss you on the mouth." They looked horrible. They were talking to me, but I couldn't understand what they were saying. They were crying. Some of them ran out of the compound and into the street.

It turned out that most of the people around us were not Jews. Rather than let us have them, most of the Jews had been killed a few hours before we got there. The Germans knew we were close, so they had killed them. I just didn't understand it. The survivors we were seeing were political prisoners, gypsies, and all kinds of other people the Nazis had considered misfits.

I couldn't take it all in. Less than a year before, I had been going to Franklin High School. I had been fighting for months. The whole idea was to survive. Get this over with and don't get killed. Fight the enemy, and the Germans are our enemy. That was my frame of mind. What I was seeing didn't have the impact on me then that it did later on. I was thinking, well, we have released all these people, so let's go. What are we supposed to do next?

I just wanted to get away from that place, away from the black and white, away from smelling death, away from all those living people who looked like they were dead. After we liberated them, a lot of them just went out into the village of Dachau. There were houses right across the street from the camp. German people were all around, but they denied knowing anything about what went on in the camp.

We went over to the so-called infirmary and hospital. Dead people were lying on the wooden slats they used for beds. Some of the people who were still alive were too weak to get up. We went back toward the northeast corner of the camp, opposite from where we'd seen the boxcar full of bodies. There was a little gate, which went to a building outside the walls. That was the crematorium. They had a room in there with all these bodies ready to be burned.

There was a room called a brausebad, which means shower-bath. The prisoners would be told they were going there to take a bath before they were sent to someplace better. They would take off all their clothes, and then they'd be gassed in the room where they were expecting to get a shower.

We stayed there about two or three days. We slept in some of the barracks that the German soldiers had occupied. Before we left we went out into an open field. It was cold. The order was, "Take off all your clothes." We did, and they sprayed us with something new called DDT. I had never heard of that before. Then they shaved all the hair off our bodies to keep us from getting the fleas that carried typhus fever. That was killing a lot of those people who were in the camp, and it was the reason they said not to let the prisoners kiss you on the mouth. We were given some clothes that were not new, but they were fresh. Then we rejoined our outfit.

Munich had already fallen, and we moved on to Tittmoning, which is on the Zalzach River on the border of Czechoslovakia. We were preparing to go into Czechoslovakia when the war ended. We were glad the war was over, but we didn't yell or shout or jump up and down. We just started hunting us a place to take a bath, find a toothbrush if we could, or get some hot food. We cleaned ourselves

up the best way we could, and we had a picture of ourselves taken on the day the war ended. We thought we were all clean, but we

The day the war ended. I'm at the very back on the far right.

were really a cruddy looking bunch. We also got together and prayed to thank God for taking care of us.

MARKING TIME

Chapter Fifteen

When the war ended we had not taken a bath for months, and our uniforms were stiff on us since we had been in them so long. But you could get a German housewife to wash all your clothes—shirt, pants, and everything you had—for two bars of soap. She would use one bar to wash your clothes, and she would keep the other one. So we started having cleaner clothes.

Day after the war is over.

Pretty soon they sent us to Austria, and we began to train to go fight in Japan. Then the two Atomic bombs we dropped put an end to the war. I believe over a million people would have likely been killed invading Japan,

Entering Austria.

so I supported the decision to drop those bombs. One of the best things about the war being over was that I finally got to drink milk again. Charlie Theisen and I found a creamery, and we brought a big container of milk back to our squad. We stayed in Austria, and we moved from village to village until we finally settled in a little village called Stumm. We were sent there to search for war criminals. We weren't looking for regular German soldiers. We just told them the war was over. We told them to surrender their weapons and go home. We were after Nazis and war criminals.

One of our guys could speak German fluently, and he would put on civilian clothes and go up into the mountains and pretend that he was a German. He would stay up there three or four days and find out if there was anybody we needed to get. He would come back down and say somebody is at this house or that house. Then we would go up where he had been and bring them out. They usually weren't too shocked or afraid.

One time I found an Austrian who had been in the German army. His name was Toni, and he was about the same age I was. I found him up in the mountains and brought him down to Stumm to be interrogated. Toni was very scared. He had heard a lot of propaganda about how the American soldiers killed and tortured their captives. The officer in charge thought he was a Nazi, but I didn't think he was so I stood up for him, and the officer finally said Toni could go home.

So we stayed in Stumm, and we were finally getting some time off. We even got to play some ping-pong and volleyball. While we were in Stumm, I was chosen to be a member of a drill platoon representing the 232nd Infantry Regiment. I liked learning all the

Practicing drills

fancy drills. We had a competition, and we beat drill platoons from the 222nd and 242nd Regiments, so we were invited to lead the May Day parade in Vienna. We went by truck, but the Russians stopped us as we were going in, and they made us stay in a building for awhile. We finally got where we were going and we led the parade that circled the plaza. I was proud to be the one carrying our flag. The Russians stopped our trucks all the time. I had thought they were on our side. I didn't know anything about communism at that time, but that got me to thinking.

Then we moved on to some other villages. Our commander, General Harry Collins, invited about thirteen of us to dinner just outside Salzburg, and we ate in the same house where *The Sound of Music* would be filmed twenty years later.

While we were in Austria, I was called by the company commander. He wanted me to take twenty-four men to Genoa, Italy. We were supposed to guard the shipments of wheat and flour that were coming off our ships there and moving on by rail to Vienna.

The trains had to pass through a zone controlled by the Russians, who were sidetracking the cars and stealing all of the flour and wheat. While I was in Genoa, my orders were to report to the port office, pick up the proper papers for boxcar numbers, and get the lead seals that would be used to secure the doors of each boxcar after the wheat and flour was loaded.

We would send five or six guys with live ammunition on each train, and their orders were not to let any cars off that train. We sent out trains three or four times over a two-week period, but I was only on the last train we were ordered to guard. We were on our way back to Austria, and sure enough, the Russians stopped our train. They said  one of the train wheels was too hot, and they wanted us to pull it off. We just ignored them. The engineer fired the engine up and we left. They tried to stop us again, but we finally made it into Vienna.

Another time when my unit was together, my name was called out along with three others. We were sent to Feldkirchen, Austria, which was in the French Occupation Zone. We were to spend two weeks with the French Army, while some French soldiers spent two weeks in the American Army. Feldkirchen was a beautiful place. We had lots of time on our hands, so one night after dinner the four of us played penuckle. A couple of hours later I had won all the money they had. I remembered playing marbles for keeps and how Mama had said that was wrong. I gave them all their money back, and they just didn't understand why I had.

We had a stockade for political prisoners near Salzburg called Camp Marcus Orr. The prisoners were not regular soldiers, but high officials. I would take them over to Salzburg each morning in a truck to cut meat, and to get bread, apple butter, and cheese. My job was to gather all that food up and bring it back to camp. The pieces of cheese were as big as automobile tires. The prisoners would walk on the bread with their bare feet, because it was a hard-crust bread. I would watch them cut meat and sausage, and they would hide some of it in their shirts and take  it back with them. I didn't stop them from doing it. I traded one of them some cigarettes for a handmade cigar box he made for me with pocketknives.

The best known individual we caught was Leni Riefenstahl. Leni Riefenstahl was the producer of a landmark propaganda film called *Triumph of the Will*. She produced it for Adolph Hitler. She was picked up in the Tyrolean Alps. It was not really a case of capturing her. She was up there hiding out, but she was not vicious or anything like that. She had been part of the movement that Hitler had led. She was held for a while, but she was released a little bit later on.

One day in the spring of 1946, while we were operating a POW camp at Hallein, Austria, I stopped at the company bulletin board and read a notice from the War Department. It stated that if you had immediate kin who had been killed in action, you no longer had to serve overseas. I went straight in to my company commander and told him I was eligible to go home. I was a staff sergeant by that time, and he said he would make me a top sergeant if I would stay. I told him I wanted to go home. He said he didn't blame me.

The commanding officer gave me my orders the next day, and he said to call the motor pool to send a jeep. The jeep driver came over to pick me up and he said, "Where are you from?" I said, "Franklin, Tennessee." He said, "Well, I'm from West Memphis. Why don't you go by plane?" So he drove me to the army airport, and I went in and asked if I could get a flight home. I could only take one of my bags on board, and I left the bags I couldn't take with the jeep driver. There was also a limit on how much money you could take home. I had accumulated a lot of money from selling cigarettes and liquor rations, but you could only have your salary and a small percentage extra, so I gave him several hundred dollars. I just wanted to get on that plane.

It was one of those paratrooper-type planes with the seats facing each other. There were colonels and other high-ranking officers on board. I had never flown before. We flew to Frankfurt to get fuel, then we flew on to Paris, and everybody got off the plane. I went down into Paris with all of the officers, and we went into this big building and found bunks.

The next morning I was hungry, and I rode an underground train out to the edge of Paris to get breakfast. After I ate it hit me that I didn't know how to get back. I was walking down the street in what I hoped was the right direction when two MPs came up in a truck and stopped me. They checked my orders because there were a lot of soldiers who were absent without leave in Paris. I told them I had a brother who was killed and how I was eligible to go home. I told them I was trying to get to the train station. One of them had also had a brother killed in Italy, and they took me to the train station.

From Paris I went to Le Havre, where I waited a couple of days before I boarded a Liberty ship, the USS New Yorker, and left for New York City. I didn't get sick on the way back because the sea was calm. There were a lot of other guys going back, too, and the main thing we did was watch the only film they had, *A Bell for Adano*, with Anthony Quinn, about twelve times.

It only took us five or six days to make the crossing back to New York City. From there we went by train to Camp Kilmer, New Jersey, which I had come through a year-and-a-half earlier on my way to Europe. They served us a big homecoming meal at Camp Kilmer, and then we went on by train to Camp Atterberry, Indiana. When we got there, they asked us where we wanted to be stationed while we were waiting to be discharged. When I saw the choices, I knew where I wanted to go. Rebecca had no idea I was so close to home, and when I called her and said I would be in Clarksville, Tennessee the next day she was awfully surprised. I believe she shed a few tears.

Back Home

Chapter Sixteen

Rebecca, Dorthy, Frances, and Bobby were all waiting for me when I got to Clarksville at about three in the morning. I remember taking Rebecca's hand. Her hand felt so small to me. I had stayed in love with her the whole time I was away, but all I had been able to do was write her letters and do things like send her roses from Vienna and candy from Salzburg. The young man who had proposed to Rebecca before she and I fell in love had never given up on the idea of marrying her. He had come back from the service while I was still in Europe, and he had done his best to win Rebecca back. I'm sure that was hard for her, but she was steadfast in her commitment to me, and she turned him down. We drove down to Nashville, and then we came on down

Rebecca

131

Franklin Road. I was so glad to get back to Mama. She had a big breakfast waiting for us. It was early May, 1946. I was home.

Franklin looked pretty much the way it had looked when I left. There were still eight grocery stores on Main Street. The school was there. My church was there. The houses and businesses were all right where they had been. But the thing that was different was that when you looked around, my friend Bobby Akin was not there. He had been killed in action in Germany. Scobie Burchett was not there. Beverly Chadwell was not there. Jack Reynolds was not there. Boots Redmon was not there. Mack Terry

was not there. And my brother David was not there either.

So Franklin had changed in a very basic way. Over 100 young men from Franklin and Williamson County had not come home. That had more of an impact on me than anything else. And guys like Roy Barker had come back, but he only had the partial use of his arm. I knew how lucky I was to have taken part in that war and gotten home alive and in one piece. And, of course, I had changed, too. I was much more mature than I was when I left. I realized what death meant. I had learned that the world was a lot bigger and more varied than I had realized.

I had two or three days before I had to report to Camp Campbell. People at home did not treat me differently, but they were glad to see me—they were glad to see all of us. I knew everybody, and there were a lot of questions.

After a few weeks at Camp Campbell, I went to Fort Bragg, North Carolina to be discharged. There was a whole room full of soldiers, and some officer told me if I would join up, some of the others would join up, too. I told him I just wanted to go back home. So I was discharged, but I found there was going to be a wait before I could get a train back to Nashville.

Alva Jefferson, one of my friends from Franklin, had gotten out at the same time, and we took a bus to Chattanooga from Fort Bragg. We were going to hitchhike on to Nashville, and we stood out on the side of the road for a long time, but not one car came by. Finally a construction truck drove up and the guy told us the road had been closed for months.

He took us over and got us a ride on another truck. On our way to Nashville we were riding in the bed of this truck, and there was a car behind us. We mouthed where we wanted to go, the guy in the car nodded, and we tapped on the back window of the cab. The driver let us out, we rode on to Nashville, and got home to Franklin from there.

I married Rebecca on August 28, 1946, at the First Presbyterian Church on Main Street in Franklin. Rebecca was a member of the First Presbyterian Church, and Henry Mobley was the pastor who married us. It was a formal wedding, and Rebecca wore a long gown with a train. My brothers and Henry Cannon were the groomsmen, and Rebecca had her friends as the bridesmaids. I was still kind of an introvert, and there I was up in front of all those people.

I was sweating and nervous, and a fly came and lit on my forehead, and he kept on crawling around. I wanted to shoo him away, but I thought I had better not move. So I was standing there, the fly was crawling all over my face, and my eyes were rolling around until Henry Cannon stepped over and shooed him away. I don't know if anyone laughed, but at least I was able to successfully say, "I do."

Our wedding day

We had a reception down at Rebecca's house, and since we didn't have an automobile, nobody could tie tin cans on the back. But my brother-in-law Baxter Ewing, my sister Dorthy's husband, had an automobile. He said you all come on and change your clothes, and we will just go for a ride. So we drove down to Columbia and all around, and then we came back after things had died down. Later that night we caught a train at Union Station in Nashville. The train was called the *Azalean*, and it took us down to New Orleans, by way of Mobile, for our honeymoon. So we spent our wedding night on that train. When we got back, I started getting ready to go to college on the GI bill. I never agreed with a lot of government giveaways, but I felt like the sacrifices our soldiers made for the war effort justified the GI bill.

I had been approached about playing college football when I was finishing high school, and when I came out of the army, Vanderbilt wanted me to come there. Dr. Guffee was an alumnus, and he really wanted me to go to Vanderbilt. So I went to practice, and Red Sanders was the coach. When I was in high school I weighed about 185 pounds, but I only weighed about 160 pounds when I got out. I had lost a lot of weight and strength, my legs weren't strong, and I just wasn't into playing. So I told Vanderbilt I didn't want to stay.

Coach Sanders said the coach up at Tennessee Tech was a friend of his, and maybe I should go up there. The coach, Putty Overall, called me and I transferred to Tennessee Tech. Rebecca and I moved to Cookeville, and we stayed with a nice man named Dr. Howard until we moved into an apartment in a building they had for veterans. The freshman coach was a guy named Wilbur Tucker, and he and I hit it off really well. I had been a pretty good high school football player, but I wasn't a star anymore. I was just going through the motions by then.

Boom Boom Cunningham was our center and we were scrimmaging one day. Boom Boom was a mean guy. He was a veteran and I think he was shell-shocked or something. I was playing linebacker, and as I was making a play, he hit me in the mouth with his elbow. One of my teeth was hanging out of my mouth. I started to reach for it, but Coach Overall was there and he said not to pull on it. They took me in my uniform over to the dentist, and he put it back in. He saved the tooth and I've still got it, but it turned dark.

The experience of playing football at Tennessee Tech was the same as it had been at Vanderbilt—I was just not into it. Maybe my body wasn't ready for a lot of extra physical work yet. Maybe I should've relaxed a little bit longer before I came back out. Going right back into it was a mistake. Back in high school the big game on Friday night was all you thought about—how we were going to really get after whoever we were playing. But I'd gone through a lot of things in the war. I'd seen a lot, and I just couldn't get fired up about playing football. It didn't make much difference to me after that.

I came home from Cookeville for a visit in the spring of 1948. I went out to see Mr. Yates, who was out in his field working. He said, "What do you plan on doing?" I said, "I hope to teach and coach some day." He said, "Well, our coach has resigned and we don't have anybody for next year. If you're interested, go up and talk to Mr. Thompson." So I talked to Mr. Thompson and he said he needed to talk it over with Mr. Yates. The next day they called me and said they wanted me to be the coach of the football team for the coming season.

I only had two years of college, but they said they could get me a temporary teaching certificate, and I could transfer to Peabody College in Nashville. I would go to school at Peabody in the morning, catch the bus around noon, and get to Franklin in time to teach some PE classes before practice. I wasn't just taking over football, I was also going to be coaching basketball and baseball. Franklin High School did not have a long winning tradition when it came to football. The 1947 team had won just one game, and I only had four guys who had earned letters coming back from that team. I didn't have any parent pressures. Both Billy King's father, William King, and Gilbert Sullivan, who had three sons on my team, told me pretty much the same thing. They said, "Coach, if you have any trouble, whip my boy and send him home. Then I'll whip him, too." Of course I never had to do anything to those boys. I was twenty-two years old. I wasn't a whole lot older than some of my players.

136

We got started in the middle of August, and there was one thing I did right off that was downright stupid, and everybody else did it, too. In those days coaches thought that players didn't need water when they were practicing. We would be out in the heat, and instead of giving them water, we gave them salt tablets. They were losing water all the time, and I'd give out salt tablets because that's what everybody else did. Don't give them any water. Make them tough. Its a wonder we didn't kill them. Later on we learned to furnish water the whole time they were practicing.

I really was not prepared to be a head coach. I was doing what I wanted to do, but I didn't know how to do it. All I knew was to do it as hard as I could. I remember the first football game we played. We lost to Sparta 66 to 6. We had some younger players who I thought would end up being really good, and we improved as the year went on.

One of the hardest things I ever had to do in my life happened early in that first football season. I had to go meet the train that

Dan, me, Bobby, and William

brought the remains of my brother David back to Franklin. The four surviving Gentry brothers—William, Dan, Bobby, and I—went to the depot and waited for the train. Pretty soon we could hear the whistle off in the distance. It had such a mournful sound. We got the flag-draped casket. Then we had the funeral, and David was buried at Mount Hope Cemetery. It was hard for everybody in the family, and it was especially hard for Mama, but she finally had all five of her boys back home.

FRANKLIN HIGH SCHOOL

Chapter Seventeen

I had started my teaching career about three weeks after our first football practice. On the first day of school I didn't know anything about what I was doing. Before the students came in, I was sitting there just looking at papers and books. I didn't know what to do first. Miss Johnnie Baugh, who had taught at Franklin as far back as just about anybody could remember, came in and picked up my roll book and said, "Come on with me." She made it out for me and told me how to do things. She would always check on me, and that helped me get off to a good start.

I would have class at Peabody every morning at 8 o'clock, and I would get out about noon, and since I didn't have a car, I'd catch the bus back out to Franklin. I would teach PE classes in the afternoon, and then we'd have football practice. Our football team had a rough start, but we ended up winning a couple of games toward the end of our season, so things were turning around. We were a lot better in basketball—we won all but two of our games, and we also had a pretty good baseball season.

Rebecca and I had moved into a house on Fifth Avenue, and three or four weeks after the end of school, our first son, Jim Jr., was born. The next year I was still riding into Nashville on the

Interurban bus and going to Peabody, then coming back in the afternoons to teach PE and coach. The first year I had coached by myself, but before we started the 1949 season I got David Johnston and my younger brother Bobby to be assistant coaches. They both were a big help, and over the years there were other coaches like Ernest McCord who did a great job with the players we had.

I started to pick up a lot of things I could do better as a coach. There were techniques I wish I had known in the beginning, but that isn't the way it works. You don't begin with experience. You have to pick it up as you go. We only won twice in my second season, but nobody really embarrassed us, and our program began improving. One reason that athletics were getting better in Franklin was the development of the County Center. It was down behind the high school, and it had a lot of functions, but the main one was as an arena for horse shows. There were also tennis courts, and the field was used by my high school teams for both football and baseball. Mr. Yates had brought the community leaders together and spearheaded the whole thing. He got me to run it, and one of the reasons it became successful was because of the work my brother, Bobby, did there. The County Center was a gathering place for kids in the summer, and after we got a Little League baseball program started there, just about every boy in Franklin was playing baseball.

I was still coaching basketball too, and basketball was the big sport in places around Williamson County like Hillsboro and College Grove and Bethesda. They each had a high school, but they weren't big enough to have a football team or a baseball team. When basketball season came, boy, everybody would go to those games. And those county schools didn't like Franklin one bit. They were going to beat those smart aleck city slickers from town.

They had these little gyms that would be so crowded, people would take up part of the court. At Hillsboro we usually played games on an oval floor. There would be ten or fifteen men here, and ten or fifteen over there, and in all four corners, so we were left with an oval. You couldn't shoot from the corner because you couldn't get to the corner. You had to play right up and down the middle of the floor, and they would set up a zone defense and there wasn't any way you could get anybody near the basket.

I remember playing once at Bethesda, where they had a big potbellied stove in the corner to heat the gym. They would pile the coal in there and fire it up. Somebody threw a long pass that night and hit the stovepipe and knocked it down. Smoke was filling the gym, so we had to call the game off for a while. I was threatened one time at Bethesda. The game was over and a man at the door had his knife open and he said, "You're not leaving here." And I said, "Whoa here, I don't know about that." I didn't try to challenge him, and then somebody came along and got him away. He was just some old man who was mad because we had won the game.

After I got my degree from Peabody, I also started teaching biology, but football was still growing on me. When my brother Bobby came to teach at Franklin, I turned over the basketball team to him and that helped me as a football coach. I think I had the basics for being a good coach, and to me that meant wanting to get the most out of a player that I could.

Some of what I tried to do as a coach, I had learned from Sergeant LaCaze back in basic training. Just stay on him until he does what you want him to—until he does everything he possibly can. I feared Sergeant LaCaze at first, but he had known what we needed. He was hard on us, but I learned that you can't think of yourself only as an individual. You are responsible for yourself, but you are part of a team. You have to hold up your end of the deal. That is the way I tried to coach. It boiled down to responsibility. You are responsible for blocking this guy. You are responsible for being in position to make a tackle. Most of that came from being in the service. I ended up having great respect for Sergeant LaCaze.

I knew that there was a limit to what a guy could do, but I also felt that if he wanted to do something badly enough, he could do it. I tried to get that idea into my players every chance I could. I'd say, "You have got to want to do this," and then I'd challenge them to do it. Sometimes the other coaches and I might be comical in the way we went about it. Two guys might be going against one another and we'd say, "Do you know what he has been saying about your mother?" He knew it wasn't true, but sometimes it got his adrenaline going. You have to sprinkle in a little humor along the way, a little love along the way, but you also have to stay on a player to get as much out of him as you can. Some of that went back to service, too. The other guys didn't expect you to fall down and wait for somebody else to do it. You were expected to do your job. It helped me to have learned that.

The fact that I had played athletics had helped me during the worst part of the fighting, and being in the war helped me as a coach. I was responsible for myself. Nobody else was responsible for me. I only remember one guy who we didn't respect in the war, and we didn't respect him because he wouldn't pull his load. He looked for ways to get out of doing things. We didn't want him around us because we couldn't trust him.

I didn't read up much on football. Most of what I learned about new strategies was by doing and by talking to other coaches. Coach J. B. Akin, who had coached for a year with Mr. Yates when I played at Franklin, was at BGA and he used a formation that was called the Split-T. He put in the Split-T, and when I saw that I said, "Wait a minute. Our quarterback can do that." Our quarterback was Crawford Alexander, and he did a great job of running the Split-T. We had good enough backs to run it, so we ended up being pretty mean with that Split-T. I learned that from Coach Akin, and then I changed our defense, too.

Back then almost everybody had been running the same defense, a 6-2-2-1. But then they started changing. I went from a six-man front to a five-man front—it was commonly called the Eagle defense. I made some changes in the way we'd line up, and later on we started going to football camp. I might have been one of the first coaches in the area to take a football team to camp. I think the first one we went to was at Standing Stone Park, up in Overton County.

I would hire a couple of cooks, buy all the food, and we would load up in trucks or whatever we had, and go off and spend a week at camp.

The program built up every year. I was learning as the players were learning, and our other coaches were making a big difference. In 1951 we had one of the best teams Franklin High School had ever had. After we lost our opening game, we went on to win ten games in a row. I always thought

With 1951 Captains
Floyd Hunter and Billy King.

that I learned more from my players than I taught them. The best part of coaching was when I could make a guy really get after it.

1951 Franklin High School Football Team.

143

When that happened I felt successful. He might not have done it right, but if he really fought and found a way to do his job, I was happy. I didn't get too nervous before the games. If I'd done my job on Monday, Tuesday, Wednesday, and Thursday, then we should be all right on Friday night.

Every season was full of stories, and one of the funniest stories that I can think of is when we were playing the old Tennessee Industrial School. Joe Sills was the coach at that time.

He was a good guy. We had a fine team that year, and his team wasn't very good. Back then a substitute could go off the field anywhere he wanted to. Coach Sills sent in a sub, and the boy he  replaced came out on our side, and stayed down at the end of our bench. He just stayed there with our players. I kept seeing him down there, and I finally told somebody, "Find out what that boy is doing down there." He came back and said, "Coach, he is going to stay over here because he's afraid if he goes back on the other side, his coach is going to put him back in the game."

 Once we had a game at Mount Pleasant, and we had lost our quarterback and gone back to the single wing. Our center, Floyd Hunter, got confused and was afraid to snap the

ball. Everybody took off anyway, and Floyd ran about fifteen yards downfield and handed the ball to the official. The official took the ball and signaled first down.

Another night we played at Dickson County and it was a pretty good rivalry. They got ahead of us right off, but we came back and beat them. Their field was down in a bowl, and I remember coming up those steps when we were leaving. I got almost to the top, and this man stepped up in front of me and put his hands on my chest, and then he pushed me back. He said, "You're not going anywhere." Ernest McCord was right behind me carrying his clipboard. Ernest was very mild mannered. There was a lady standing there, and he said, "Ma'am, hold this clipboard. I think I am going to have to fight." That guy decided to move out of the way and we went on. I think he knew that Ernest meant business. It wouldn't have been a good idea to have a fight with Ernest.

Ernest McCord

A few years later we were playing at Dickson, and Ken Frost, whose nickname was "Baby" because he had several older brothers, was probably our best player. Baby had what we called a knock-down shoulder because it would get dislocated from time to time. When that happened I would go out on the field, take my shoe off, put my foot underneath his arm, and pull the shoulder back in place and he would just keep on playing.

Baby Frost had the reputation of being a pretty rough player, and one night at Dickson he did something and they threw him out of the game. He was over on the sidelines with me and his shoulder pads were off. Dickson had the ball and they were running a play right toward us. I had my hand on Baby's shoulder, and all of a sudden I felt him leave. He went on the field without his pads or his helmet and he hit the ball carrier. He knocked the boy down, the boy fumbled, and Baby ran back and sat down right under my arm. The officials never knew what had happened. One of the Dickson

145

players kept pointing, but he didn't know who to point at. Baby played college football at Tennessee, and went on to play professional football with the Dallas Cowboys and the Cleveland Browns. And it wasn't his shoulder that finally ended his career, it was his knee.

One of the biggest changes that came to football in my early years of coaching was facemasks on helmets. Facemasks changed the way we taught tackling. Before they came along you tackled with your shoulder, but then you started putting your head into the ball carrier's body. There were fewer broken noses and knocked-out teeth, but there were more neck injuries. It gave players a lot more confidence to have that facemask on since they knew they wouldn't get hit in the face.

After two or three years at Franklin High School, I finally got my first automobile. Some of the students were probably wondering what was wrong with me, not having a car. But I didn't have one growing up, I hadn't needed one in the army, and living over on Fifth Avenue, I could walk to school. But I finally went ahead and got my driver's license and bought an automobile. We were still living over on Fifth Avenue when Rebecca had our second son,

Allen, in the summer of 1952. I was running Willow Plunge during the summers, and I was able to give jobs to some of the kids from the high school.

Sometime around 1953 it was decided that there wouldn't be any more spring football practices. I called a meeting of the football players and told them I had good news and bad news. The

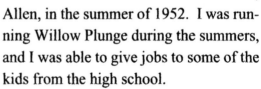

good news was no football in the spring. The bad news was that we were going to have a track team, and they were all on it. When I started the track team, I gave up baseball and my brother Bobby took over the team. We ended up having some really good performers in track. Robert Inman, Wayne Inman, Tandy Rice, Chick Irvin, and Porter Maxwell were some of our best competitors. Robert had gotten an old cane pole out of a roll of carpet, and he had been vaulting across a creek. He always pole vaulted barefooted, and he

ended up being State Champion and going to Tennessee Tech on scholarship.

What was true of teaching was the same as it was with coaching—things were happening all the time and there were lots of stories. One story I would like to forget happened in my second year at Franklin. One morning I went in the gymnasium upstairs and I opened a window to let in a little fresh air. Mr. Thompson was down there on the south side of the building next to the Carter House, and just as I opened the window he looked up and said, "Coach, come down here. I need you." When I went down, he was standing beside what I thought was a football dummy. It was a young woman from out of town who had been

murdered, and her body was dumped beside the school. The people she had supposedly been trying to blackmail were eventually caught and sent to prison.

That happened back in 1949, and it was the only gruesome thing that ever happened. Most things were funny. We had a teacher named Mrs. Dedman, and the students had nicknamed her War Horse. Some of them thought she was mean. She didn't like her nickname. One day somebody was putting on a little carnival down in the basement, and one of the attractions was a mechanical horse you put money in and it rocked back and forth. A boy named Robert Underwood was riding the horse and he was yelling out, "Whoa, horse! Whoa, Horse!" Mrs. Dedman was near enough to hear him, and she thought he was saying, "War horse! War horse!" He was a great big boy, but she got him by the ear, so his toes were almost off the ground, and she whipped him.

Mr. Daly Thompson was a wonderful man. He was a great role model and educator, but around 1955 he was forced out of his position as principal of Franklin High School. There were some new people at the school board, and they wanted to make some changes. They forced out a man who was unbelievably good, but he went on to benefit BGA.

On the morning of January 29, 1956, a bolt of lighting hit Franklin High School and set it on fire. Ernest McCord and I got to school about the same time, and part of it was blazing. All the records were inside, and we thought we might be able to save them. So we went up and broke down the door, and ran in and got the file cabinets. As we were coming out the front door, the papers on the bulletin

board beside us were already burning. We took the cabinets out on the sidewalk, and then we set them down. It was raining and somebody said, "Those papers are going to get wet. You'd better take them over to that porch across the street to keep them dry." We couldn't pick them back up. We had to get help. That shows what adrenaline will do. The next day the fire was out, but there was still water dripping in what was left of the building. The library had burned, but there was one picture left on the wall that had survived the fire—a picture of Mr. Thompson.

The gymnasium didn't burn and its basement was partitioned off, and we had some classes down there. We also used the Sunday School rooms of some of the local churches until a new high school could be built. We spent almost two years in the basement of the gym and in those church classrooms. It got pretty crowded, and it also got a little more crowded in our house on Fifth Avenue after our third son, Scott, was born in the spring of 1957. In December of that same year we moved into our new building on Hillsboro Road, and Franklin High School had a new campus.

After we had been there awhile, a female PE teacher came to me and said, "Coach, I think some of your football players are peeping through a hole into the girls' dressing room." I said, "Well, I'll take care of that right now." The players were already in the locker room dressing. I told David Johnston, who was one of my coaches, "We'll just take them out to the field and talk to them." So we went out and had them all gathered around in a circle and I said, "Now before we start, I understand somebody has been peeping through a hole in the girls' dressing room. If you have been doing that, you go on back in and I will come in and we will talk about it." Finally one or two got up, and then more got up, and that kept on until David Johnson and I were the only ones left out on the field. I went back in and I think I just told them I didn't want them doing that again.

I still loved being around kids, and the football program was going along pretty well. I had some great players like Ned Sullivan, Ray Dalton, Albert Posnak, and Billy Speck, but even though we were still going to bowl games, I was losing my enthusiasm to coach. I thought I was losing control of what it took to run a good athletic program. The attitude of the administration, and of the principal in particular, was more and more of a problem.

It got to the point that if I wanted to order uniforms, I couldn't. If I wanted to get tape so we could wrap the players' ankles before games, I would have to go ask for tape, and then I wouldn't be given enough to do the job. I couldn't do things the way I wanted, and by the end of the 1961 season I had gotten tired of fighting the whole situation. I didn't want to be part of it anymore. I thought I should give up coaching. So I went to Mr. Yates, who was the Superintendent of Schools, and I told him how I felt. He said, "Don't make your decision right off. Let's think about it for a few days."

In the meantime, Mr. J. B. Akin at BGA heard about my situation and he called and said he wanted to come and talk to me. We got together and he asked if I would consider coming to BGA. I talked to the Headmaster, Mr. Paul Redick, and I decided I would leave Franklin and go to BGA. So I went back and told Mr. Yates that I was gone.

OLD WAYS AND BGA

Chapter Eighteen

Not too long before I left Franklin High School, we moved from our house on Fifth Avenue to a home we built out on Murfreesboro Road, in what had been the orchard on the farm where we lived when my daddy died. We had been living in town, and I had been busy teaching and coaching and helping Rebecca raise our three sons, but I continued to do a lot of hunting and fishing and trapping. As I grew older, I'd gotten pretty skilled at trapping. I think the biggest catch I ever had

Jim, Scott, Allen, Dandy, and Tippy

was thirty-six muskrats in one night. My brother Dan and I got a boat, and we had to travel a good long way to get that many. I think it was around the same time that we trapped two hundred muskrats and forty or fifty mink in one year. That meant big money then.

Mr. Chester Williams lived way back in the woods, and he would let Dan and I trap on the creek where he lived. One morning  we were going down to see what we had caught and he said, "I believe I'll go with you boys." In the very first trap we had a big old coon, but he said, "I want that." We gave it to him because it was on his place, but we hated to give up that hide. The next morning we went back, and he came out and said, "When you boys come back, we'll have breakfast." So we came back up after checking our traps. He had skinned the coon the night before, and he gave us the hide. He had barbecued the coon, and we had the best breakfast of barbecued coon, scrambled eggs, biscuits, and pear preserves we ever put in our mouths.

I hunted and fished with people other than Dan. When I first started to coach, I bought my equipment from Jimmy Eanes, who sold sporting goods in Nashville. We got to be close friends. He loved to fish, and we taught him how to limb line. I also did some fishing with Buddy Mills, who was the principal of the junior high school in Franklin.

One day Buddy and I were going limb lining, and we went out to catch some minnows. We went out to Hamilton's Creek, about four miles out Lewisburg Pike, where I knew we could catch some good minnows. We were going through a pasture, and up on the hillside there was a bull. Well, Buddy could not keep his eyes off that bull. He was scared of the bull, and he kept asking whether he was going to come after us or not. I'd tell him the bull wasn't going to bother us, but Buddy was still nervous. We got in the water, and we began to catch the minnows in our seine. We got to where we only needed to make one more sweep and we'd have all the minnows we needed. It looked like Buddy was going to stop, so I said, "Keep coming." When I said that, he bolted out of the creek and took the minnow net with him and pulled me down in the  water at the same time. We lost all the minnows, and later on he told me, "I thought you said, *he's* coming." Well, the bull was still up on the side of the hill grazing just as peacefully as he could. So we had to go back into the creek and start all over again.

Some years later Dan was with me and he said, "I just can't get anybody to go do anything with me anymore." He was just playing on my sympathy. He said, "I know where there are some big catfish under a rock, and I can't get anybody to go with me to get them out." So I said, "Well, I'll go with you." He had on a pair of old bib overalls, and he was barefooted. We went down to Bradley's Bend on the Big Harpeth, to the big rock he had been talking about. He said, "Now I'm going under, and it's going to take me awhile." I would always put my foot on him to hold him down while he was working so he wouldn't have to struggle to stay down. Just as he went under, I heard a bump, bump noise.

A canoe was coming around the bend. There were two guys with brand new hunting clothes on paddling a brand new canoe. All they could see was me standing in the water by myself. They had no idea Dan was under the water. Just as they got up to us, Dan started pinching me on the leg to let him up. He came up with mud running out his nose, ears, and mouth and gasping for breath. Those two guys had their eyes bugging out, and they started paddling just as fast as they could. They thought I was trying to drown Dan. They would paddle and look back, paddle and look back. I'll bet they went home and told some wild stories about this guy getting killed out in the river. But Dan got his fish, and we went home.

I enjoyed most of the teaching and coaching I did at Battle Ground Academy. It didn't take me too long to realize that it was a whole lot easier to be an assistant than it was to be a head coach. I didn't have to make a lot of decisions, and I didn't have to put up with a lot of the things that came with being a head coach. Our head coach was Bill Brown, and it was his first year to be in charge of a team. Mr. Redick was the headmaster at BGA, but Mr. Akin, who was the business manager, had been the one who first talked to me about coming to BGA. Mr. Daly Thompson was still on the faculty, and he taught Latin.

There were plenty of lively characters at BGA, among the students and the faculty. BGA had both day students and boarders, and some of those boarders would slip out when they weren't supposed to. One night a teacher named Bunny Akin was on duty and one of the boys was not in his room in the dormitory. So Bunny got in the boy's bed, and about 2 o'clock in the morning, the boy came back. He took off his clothes and started to get into bed. When he came across Bunny Akin, he thought there was a dead man in his bed. They could hear him screaming all over the dorm.

There was a teacher named Ralph Naylor, and one time when he was keeping study hall, some of the students hid alarm clocks in a bunch of the vacant desks. They went off every five minutes or so, and every time it happened there would be a lot of chuckling and giggling. Mr. Naylor finally had enough of alarm clocks going off, and he got up and found as many of them as he could. Then he opened up the window—the study hall was on the second floor—and he threw all the clocks down onto the concrete underneath. There were pieces of clocks everywhere. The boys whose alarm  clocks hadn't gone off yet ran to get them before he did.

I taught biology at BGA along with coaching football, and I also coached wrestling. One difference between Franklin and BGA was that at BGA the players didn't have after-school jobs, so they were more consistent about being at practice. The boys at BGA might have been a little better off than some of those at Franklin, but I never thought there was any connection between how much money a boy's family had and how good a football player he was. You'd hear things like, "He is just an old corn-fed boy who lives out on a farm. He is really tough." But some of the best players I had never lived near a farm. Being a good player comes from what is in a boy's heart and what his abilities are, so money didn't make a lot of difference. I appreciated some of those early guys who would cut tobacco all-day and then come on in to practice football in the afternoon. They would show up with no shirt and be sweaty and dirty and go out and practice. They were tough, but there were some others just as tough who didn't do any of that.

I was an assistant coach under Bill Brown, and I had become athletic director by the time he left after the 1965 season. When I followed him as head coach, I took over a very talented team with players like George Silvey, Robert Akin, Steve Robinson, Don Denbo, Harry Ford, Brother Campbell, Ralph McCracken, and Jack Milam.

Before the start of the 1966 season, our second team offense was running plays against our first team defense. Dickie Arnold was playing quarterback, and on one of the plays he got knocked up in the air and into some bushes that were growing beside the practice field. Dickie finally staggered out of the bushes and I turned to my brother, Bobby, who was coaching with me. I said we either had the worst second team in the country, or the best first team. I sort of kept it to myself, but I thought we could go undefeated.

We didn't get too much attention at first, but then we beat Deshler, the top team in Alabama. The players did everything that was asked of them, and they really came together as a team. We didn't lose a regular season game, and we ended our season by beating Crossville, which was ranked fifth in the state, 43-7 in the Tobacco Bowl. We were named State Champions, and I had really wanted that for our team. They had sacrificed a lot and they deserved it. It was a great year, but I had only agreed to coach for one season. When we got through I told Mr. Akin, "Well, that's it." He didn't understand and it was hard for him to accept, but I'd made up my mind.

1966 Undefeated BGA Wildcats.

Bill Cherry took over as head coach, and he brought in a young assistant coach named Carlton Flatt, who had been an assistant up at Tennessee Tech. The first time I met Coach Flatt was in the locker room in the basement of the BGA gym. He was young, aggressive, and very eager to learn. Bill Cherry resigned after one season, and Mr. Akin hired Marvin Franklin, who had played at Vanderbilt. After two or three weeks of practice, Coach Franklin didn't think much of the athletic ability of the team, and he resigned. I offered the job to Bill Cherry, who had become an assistant coach, and I also offered it to Carlton Flatt, but neither one of them would take it, so I ended up with the job again. The kids fought hard, but we had a terrible season. We didn't win a single game. John Oxley became head coach the next year, and I was happy to go back to just being the athletic director.

I have many fond memories of BGA, from the football teams and the wrestling teams I coached, to all those years of teaching biology. All three of my sons graduated from BGA. But I had been running into the same situation I'd had back at Franklin High School. Maybe it was my fault, but it got to where I couldn't get things done like I wanted them done. It was one thing after another. While I was athletic director, I needed a head coach for the seventh and eighth grade team. I was given an English teacher who didn't seem qualified to be a coach. I said I didn't want him, but I got him anyway. I finally left BGA in 1977.

BRENTWOOD ACADEMY

Chapter Nineteen

Carlton Flatt had left BGA after a couple of years to go into business, but soon he was back into coaching. He called me one day and said, "A new school is opening down here in Brentwood. I'm going to be the coach, and I would like you to come down here and help me." I put him off for a few years. My youngest son, Scott, was at BGA, and I wanted him to stay there until he could graduate. Then Carlton called me again and he just said, "Scott graduated." So I said, "I'll come down there and talk to you," and I went on to Brentwood Academy. I continued to teach biology, just like I had at Franklin and at BGA, and after a number of years I gave up Biology and began to teach Tennessee history.

Coach Flatt and I had always thought pretty much alike. I really learned to respect his ideas and his approach. Jim Webb, another coach from BGA, also came over to Brentwood Academy. I'd put him right up at the top as far as the best people I have ever known. He really cared about kids, and he was just full of fun. So being able to work with guys like Carlton Flatt and Jim Webb was just the sort of situation I wanted to be in.

I knew Coach Flatt and he knew me, and he knew what my capabilities were. During all those years that I was at Brentwood

Academy, I would go out and do what I wanted to do. We almost always thought the same way. I could usually read his mind, and I knew what he was thinking before he said anything.

Coach Flatt's philosophy has always been to be well disciplined in every area of school, including athletics. That approach has paid off not only in wins but also, more importantly, in teaching values that stay with players for the rest of their lives. Players are expected to be on time for everything they do. They are taught to be responsible for themselves without excuses. He didn't hesitate to criticize his best players in front of the whole team, and that let everybody know there were no prima donnas.

Coach Flatt has the ability to look at the teams on the field and see the entire offense and the defense—all twenty-two players at one time. One year we were playing Loretto in the playoffs, and they were unbeaten. As soon as they lined up on defense, he saw that they'd left themselves wide open. The first play we ran was a pass from Jeff Speedy to Brad Perry, and it went for a touchdown. They didn't adjust, and the next two times we got the ball, we ran the same play on first down and scored both times. He had seen their weakness just as soon as they lined up.

Coach Flatt was smart enough to bring in some outstanding assistant coaches. He got people like Ray Dalton and Mickey Jacobs and my brother, Bobby, along with guys like John Patton and Wendell Harris. He put together coaching staffs that were hard to beat.

Back when I was 22 years old I felt like I was still a player, but as I got older I became more like a father trying to direct his children. I went from trying to stay on the same level as my players, to becoming their sole leader. I used my experience more wisely as I got older. The game of football is not for everybody, but those who really give themselves to the game can learn important lessons that aren't taught in too many other parts of our society.

The whole time I coached, I tried to teach my players where to place their feet, what foot to step with, where to put their heads, and

how to position their backs. I taught them as much as I could about their blocking assignments. Boys would ask, "Which way do I block him?" You don't block him anywhere, you just block him as he goes back and you go back with him. Some people try to turn them, but you don't turn them, you just take them away. You just take them all the way down the field if that's where they'll go. Some guys would try to step around their man and position block. That is wrong, but they learn those things over a period of time.

Football has continued to change, especially on defense. The defenses had usually been a five- or six-man front, but later on they could be anywhere from three men down to ten men down. And they moved around all the time. I coached the offensive line at Brentwood Academy, and I enjoyed the challenge of teaching blockers to read those defenses.

If the nose man was going to be blocked by the guard, or if the center was going to block the man on the guard, we used key words.

A lineman would say, "Long Arm," and what he meant was that the long arm of the law was going to reach out and get you. That is called a reach block. We didn't say reach because the people on defense might know what we meant. So "Long Arm" meant, "I'm going to block your man for you." We also used "Big Boy," which was a combination block. That came from the Big Boy Combination you could order at Shoney's Restaurant. That meant the lineman blocked a man on the line of scrimmage, and then came off that guy and onto the linebacker. A lot of times I would ask a player, "What do you think we ought to call this block?" We had "Super" and "The Price is Right," and a few other names like that. It was fun and it helped them stay interested in the game and to concentrate on what they were doing.

Another difference between my first years in coaching and later on was the difference in the size of players. Back then, if you found a boy who weighed 200 pounds, you were doing really well. Now if you find one who weighs 200, he might not even get to play because somebody else might weigh 250 or 290.

I was an assistant coach at Brentwood Academy for 22 seasons, and during that time we were State Champions eight times and well over 50 of our players signed major college football scholarships. I don't know how I could name some of them without naming all of them. Then there would be all those guys who didn't have the size or the strength or the speed or the talent, but who

1995 Brentwood Academy State Champion Football Team.

would fight you till the end of the world. Coach Flatt and I would be talking about a player and we'd say, "I'd go to war with that guy any day." That meant we trusted him. He would give us everything he had. Carlton Flatt built a winning tradition at Brentwood Academy. No Brentwood Academy team wanted to fail to uphold that tradition, and they would fight like anything to win.

As I got older my hip started really hurting me. Coach Flatt realized it and he said, "I'll tell you what, just come over and do the offense and then go home." It had gotten to the point that sometimes I would have to sit on the field in a chair to coach, and I couldn't get all the way back to the gym because I was in so much pain. Coach Flatt kept me coaching, and I was finally able to get my hip straightened out, but when he stepped down as head coach after the 1998 season, I thought it was a good time for me to retire.

High school football had kept getting more complicated with all the changing formations and defenses, and there were other changes, too. There weren't nearly as many people at ball games back when I started coaching. The intensity has changed a lot since those early days. Back then boys played more for fun. I am not saying that they didn't have fun later on, but the intensity was a lot different, and the expectations were a whole lot different than they were back when I started. It is sort of hard to put my finger on, but I think the right word is intensity.

One part of having coached for such a long time is that I have had to attend a lot of funerals of young men I cared about. I coached three brothers at Franklin: Billy, Toby, and Peter King. They were all good players. Billy went on from Franklin and played all the way through his senior year at Mississippi State. Then he came home and got a good job back here.

One night my phone rang and it was Mrs. King. She said, "Jimmy, Peter died last night." Maybe a year later, she called me again and said, "Jimmy, Toby is dead." Then their brother Billy came to see me, and after things didn't work out for him in Franklin, he moved up around Pikeville. He said, "Coach, guess what I'm doing? I am going to coach a junior high school this year." I was so proud of him. Not too long after that, Mrs. King called me again and said, "Jimmy, Billy got killed last night in an automobile accident." She had lost all three of her boys.

And Jimmy Sullivan, who was a great athlete, was killed flying a plane during the Korean War. There were so many of them down through the years. It was hard to see those lights snuffed out and gone. At Brentwood Academy we lost wonderful players like Kevin Luttrell and Crawford Smith, and we also had a great kid named Tito Lee. He was the best open-field blocker I ever saw in high school. He could get the job done. I think that Tito got to the point where he just felt like he couldn't live up to his expectations, or to the expectations of other people.

Sometimes I think the level of intensity that has been reached in high school sports is a negative. I don't approve of teams starting their practices in July and training all year round. The boys don't have time to enjoy their lives and just be boys. Now it's the same whether it is football or basketball or baseball. Kids don't get to hunt and fish and play, so I think its a mistake to have athletics take up so much time and to have everybody getting so consumed with it. You hear too many stories today where a coach is beaten up, or somebody is shot at a game, or somebody is using steroids.

GOING BACK

Chapter Twenty

Of course, what I saw at Dachau had stayed with me over the years. When I first got back, there were times when I thought I must have had a bad dream. How could what I knew I had seen be real? I even asked my mother about a letter I had written her right after I'd been to Dachau. When she said she didn't have that letter, it made me wonder about myself, but then she said my sister-in-law had it. It was a relief to know for sure that I'd seen what I'd seen—the description of Dachau in my letter was just what I remembered.

When I came back home, people had wanted me to tell war stories. I tried to talk about what had happened over there, but when it came to Dachau, I didn't do very well. I finally just quit talking about it. I got the feeling that people really didn't believe what I told them anyway. The older I got, the more emotional I got about it. I didn't talk about it at all for thirty-five years.

I was at Brentwood Academy, and it was probably in the early 1980s when there was a call for me at the school. I heard a lady's voice on the other end. She said, "Is this James C. Gentry?" I said, "Yes ma'am." "Were you in the army during World War II?" "Yes ma'am." Then she said, "Were you in the 42nd Infantry Division?" I said, "Yes ma'am." I thought, "What does this woman want?" She said, "Were you in the Two Hundred and Thirty-second Infantry?" It sounded like she was reading from something. Then she asked, "Were you in E Company?" When I said, "Yes ma'am," she said, "Then you were involved in the liberation of Dachau." I wanted to say no, but she had me. So I said, "Yes ma'am." She said, "We would like to have you come and talk to some groups in Nashville," but I said, "I can't do that." We talked and finally she said, "I understand."

The next day she called back. She said, "I understand why you don't want to do that, but would you mind putting what you saw on tape?" I told her that would be all right. So they came out and taped me telling what I'd seen. A few days later I got another phone call. This time is was a man's voice, and as soon as I heard it, I knew what he probably wanted. I could tell by the way he spoke that he must be one of the survivors. His name was Irving Lamore and he said, "I understand that you don't want to talk about it." I said, "That's right," and he said, "Would it be all right if I just came out and shook your hand?" Well, you can't turn a man down for wanting to do that, so I told him to come on out.

I remember when he drove up. I was down on the athletic field at Brentwood Academy. He got out of his car, and I went up to him. We hugged one another, and then we both started to cry. I understood why we were crying—we both knew the same thing. We sat down and we just talked and talked. Finally he said something that made me change my mind about talking about Dachau. He said, "You know, when you die you are going to take all you know with you. Nobody will ever be able to know what you saw." That made me remember the way my mother had told us stories about when she was a girl. If she hadn't done that, those things she remembered would've been lost. I went ahead and said, "I'll do it."

I struggled for the first year or two after I started telling about the Holocaust. It was too emotional. I would do all right until I got to the place where people were looking out at me through the barbed wire. Then I'd break down. I finally figured out that it was because I was facing an audience. If I was just in a room with somebody else, I was okay. But when I looked out at an audience, I'd see all those faces from years ago, looking out at me. So I learned to look up or to close my eyes when I got to that part of the story. I could tell it as long as I didn't look at those faces.

So I would give a talk and some college student would ask me, "Don't you think that it all could have been a hoax? How do you know how those people really died?" I would tell them that I really don't know what happened before I got there. I only knew what I saw. I wasn't satisfied with that answer, and I don't think they were either. The students might have thought that those people could have been sick. They could have just died of some disease before we got there. And some Germans would say, "We didn't do that. Its all propaganda."

But one day at Brentwood Academy someone said, "There's a book in the library called *Gizelle, Save the Children*." I went and I got it. It was written by a Jewish woman named Gizelle Hersh about when she was a girl. She had lived in Romania with her mother, her father, her brother, and her three sisters. The Germans came and took them to Auschwitz. Then the family was separated. They put the mother in one line, and the father and the brother in a different line. When they separated the mother from the girls, the mother told the oldest girl, "Gizelle, save the children," and that's the name of the book.

Gizelle tells how she and her sisters went from camp to camp to camp. The father, the son, and the mother didn't survive, but the girls did survive. As the Russians pushed deeper into Germany, the Americans were coming from the other direction. Finally they were caught in between, and there was almost nowhere else they could go. Then one morning the Germans told her and the others to load up—they were going to another camp. And they put all these girls and women in boxcars, and they pulled into Dachau Concentration Camp.

At the same time my unit was heading for Dachau, Gizelle was looking through a crack in the boxcar and seeing a crowd and a lot of dead bodies. They took the train out from Dachau, and later on, a train loaded with men and boys passed them on the way to Dachau. On April 30, 1945, the girls were still on the train, locked in their boxcar. Then their German guards suddenly ran away. After that there was a lot of shelling and explosions, and the buildings around them began to blow up. Planes were dropping bombs, and she was afraid that the train they were on would be hit.

After a while she looked out and saw a tank with a white star on the side. Several American soldiers came over to her boxcar and opened it up. One of them said, "Hey y'all, come on out of there." So he was from the South somewhere. It wasn't long before she found out what had happened to the men and boys who had been on the train that had passed them on its way to Dachau. A soldier told her that everybody on the train had been killed the day before—just as the camp was about to be liberated.

So I finally knew what happened just before I got to Dachau. If we had gotten there three or four hours earlier, we could have saved the boys and the men in the boxcars of that other train. But if the liberation had been a day or two later, the girls and the women might have also been killed. I knew what she had written in her book was true, because I had seen the other side of it. Everything dovetailed with what I saw. The bodies I had seen in the boxcars at Dachau were the boys and men on the train that had gone past Gizelle's train. It confirmed everything.

In 1987 Brentwood Academy gave me a sabbatical, and Rebecca and I went to Europe. I wanted to see Europe in color, not like I had seen it in the war—not in black and white and smelling bad. We went to Würzburg first. I went back to the park and found the tree where I had almost been killed. It was a weird feeling. The tree was still there, and it had healed up. We visited the Neubau Church across from where Sergeant McDavid was killed. You couldn't tell there had been a war. It was a beautiful city. They had put it all back together, and I admired them for the work they had done.

Later on we went to Stumm. I remembered a little boy who had lived there, and I went looking for him. I went over to a house, and the lady who came to the door couldn't speak English, but she pointed to a guesthouse. So we went back and there he was. He didn't remember me—he was too young, but he was very nice and he spoke English.

Then all of a sudden I saw this old lady. She had gray and red hair, and she was heading straight for me. And she wasn't walking—she was almost running. She was excited and she asked me my name. I said, "My name is Jimmy," and that's as far as I got. She said, "Jimmy Gentry." Then she started crying and laughing and jumping up and down. I thought, "What in the world? I don't know who this woman is." She was jabbering the whole time. The man who didn't remember me said, "That's my mother, Maria. She wants to have a party." Her name was Maria Hubler and she took us into her house. She put on her best dress. She had pictures made. She got on the phone and I heard her say my name. The son said, "She's talking to Toni." It wasn't long, and there came Toni. He was about my age. We hugged and it turned out that Toni was Maria's brother. He was the guy we'd taken just after the war, and I had helped get him released. She said, "You saved my Toni."

GENTRY FARM

Chapter Twenty-One

My wife Rebecca is the great-great granddaughter of Samuel Fielding Glass and his wife Sara. They established a plantation in 1848, which they named Pleasant View. They built a large two-story brick house during the 1860s, and the house and several hundred acres were eventually inherited by the next generation. By 1902 the family was living in Franklin, and tenants had moved into the house. They ended up living in only one or two rooms, and the rest of the house gradually came to be used as a barn. They would store things like corn, wheat, hay, and potatoes in there, and the house and the farm slowly became sort of a stepchild to the family. Nobody wanted to live there. Tenants kept moving in and out, and it got more and more run down as the years went by. It passed down to Mrs. Corinne Channell, Rebecca's mother, and then we became involved with the property.

George Baugh was a black man who was born around 1880 in an old log house that is still standing on our farm. He worked on the farm his whole life. George would come to town to see Mrs. Channell. He would come to the back door and take his hat off and he would say, "Miz Corinne, I need to talk to you." And she would say, "Well come on in, George." She would take him in the living room and he would say, "We are going to plant some corn down by the river, and the mule is getting kind of old." She would say, "Well George, what do you think? Do we need another mule?" He would say, "Yessum, if I could find a good one." She would say, "If you find a good one, you sell the other one and you get you a good mule." It was a little ritual they had. She always did whatever George wanted to do, and he continued to farm as long as he could. He was 96 years old when he died.

There were a couple of guys living in the house who liked motorcycles. I went out one day, and they were working on their motorcycles in one of the parlors. There was oil on the floor and they had nailed up a shelf to put some of their tools on. It was just like a garage, and it really killed me. We got rid of them, but the next tenants were also a problem. It was getting close to the time I left BGA when Rebecca and I decided to restore the house. It had electricity, but there was no indoor plumbing. It needed a huge amount of work.

Along with Rebecca and me, our sons would help when they could, but I still needed another worker. Somebody said, "If you can get Harold Cartwright, you've got a good one." I found out that was right. If Harold was supposed to be at work at seven in the morning, he would be there at about a quarter till seven. He would lay all his tools out like he was a surgeon and then start working. He would work all day and never open his mouth unless you asked him something. He never stood around. If there wasn't anything else to do, he would get up, get a broom, and start cleaning. He never stopped working. If he was doing some kind of tedious work and he didn't think he had made enough progress, he'd say, "Don't pay me much today. I didn't do too much."

One day I had some traps set way up the river and I said, "Harold, I'm going to the river, and I want you to dig a hole so we can plant a tree." I told him about the size of the tree, and I told my son Scott and some of his friends to get the tree and bring it down for Harold. I was gone for three or four hours, and when I came back the tree was not up. Harold was way down in the hole digging. The hole was about five feet deep and five feet wide and I thought he had lost his mind. I said, "Harold, what's going on?" He said, "Well, they came back with that tree, but I wasn't ready and they left. When I got finished it was too heavy to get in the hole by myself, and since I didn't have anything else to do, I just kept on digging." He gave a day's work for a day's pay and then some. There were a lot more people like that around when I was growing up.

We put in a bathroom downstairs, two bathrooms upstairs, and we also built on a little addition for our washer, dryer, and freezer. The roof had gotten old, and we had to put on a new metal roof. We would do plastering, and some of the ceilings had fallen in, so we worked hard fixing that up. We sanded and stained the floors, and we did a whole lot of painting. We took a tractor and pulled all the scrub trees and bushes away from the house. Before we did that you could hardly see the place. It took us an enormous amount of work before we moved in the house, which was somewhere around the end of 1976, and we did years of work after that.

My friendship with Ernest McCord had continued over the years, and around 1978 he called me up and said, "I've got something that I want to give you." He had dug up an oak sapling from

his backyard and wrapped up the ball in burlap. He said, "I want you to plant this, and think about me every time you see this tree." Ernest died in 1989, but that tree is about 5 1/2 feet around now. It is a sturdy, strong tree just like Ernest McCord was. I think of him every time I look at that tree. And Robert Inman, who pole-vaulted to the state championship when I coached him, brought me a shrub. Robert went into coaching and influenced a lot of young lives. He said, "Every time you see that, you are going to think of me." He passed away in

1999, but the shrub he gave me is still growing.

One spring while we were still living out on Murfreesboro Road, I planted some strawberries around a flowerbed, and I liked the way they looked. I started raising them in our garden, and when we moved to the farm, I got into the strawberry business. I found out that I could sell as many strawberries as I could raise. If I could raise 100 acres, I could sell

100 acres. But there was an awful lot of work in it. The people who came for the strawberries would ask if we had anything else. "Have you got any corn? Have you got any beans?" They wanted something else.

Our son Allen worked the farm, and he raised a variety of crops—corn, beans, wheat, and he also started raising a few pumpkins for the kids. Well, people wanted those, too. It wasn't too long before the pumpkins turned into a big time operation. Our place has now become

known as "Gentry Farm," and every October thousands of people, most of them children, come out and enjoy the beauty of fall on our farm. They walk through a cornfield maze that says Gentry Farm if it's seen from the air. They look at livestock, take a hayride, or play in one of our barns. People just love to come out here.

School groups come out, and Allen and his wife, Cindy, do a great job with them. They have classes for the children, and they ask things like how many boards it would take to replace the boards on the side of the barn, or how many square feet it would take to roof it, or how many gallons would be needed to paint it. They have the kids go out and catch insects and bring them back and talk about what they are. They go on hayrides and feed corn to the cows, and all that happens during the week. On Saturdays and Sunday afternoons the biggest crowds come in, and just about everybody leaves with a pumpkin.

Our camps got started the same way—they just sort of happened. One day while I was at BGA a mother asked me if I would keep her son with me on the farm for the summer. She said,

"I want him to enjoy farm life," and she paid me. Word got around, and I had eight campers that first year. It was just me and those eight boys. We would fish and play mumbly peg and pitch horseshoes. The next year I had about forty kids, and then it got up to sixty. I had gotten help by then, but it got to be too much, and I had to cut it back.

I was working with kids who were nine to thirteen years old, and people wanted something for younger children, so Cindy and Allen started a camp on a different part of the farm. They fixed up a camp for children who had graduated from kindergarten, but who were under nine years old. The older kids kept coming to the senior camp that I still run.

The girls and boys learn a lot about the farm and about taking responsibility for those animals that are penned up. The animals have to be watered and fed and taken care of, and the kids get to do those things. We play games in the woods like capture the flag, and they learn to hide in the bushes and sneak up on each other and all that.

They get to do so many of the things kids don't do much anymore like pitching horseshoes, swinging on rope swings, and playing mumbly peg. They also fish and swim and play in the West Harpeth River, which runs besides our farm, and they learn a little bit about limb lining, too. I think our camp has been a good thing for a lot of children.

George Baugh's first wife died, and his second wife was named Ella. Ella was a very nice lady, and before we moved out to the farm, she would see me working and bring me water and some food. But old Ella had a peg leg. I would tell the boys and girls at camp about Ella, but all they seemed to think about was her peg leg. They'd say, "Was she mean?" and I'd say, "I hadn't heard she was mean." But the first thing I knew, the old Ella story had gotten out of hand. The campers got scared of going down to the river because old Ella might get them. So one day I didn't have anything to do, and I carved "old Ella" on a tree. Pretty soon the campers found that and they said, "Look, old Ella has been here." They would see a little hole in the ground, and they thought it had been made by old Ella's peg leg. So the campers have taken it and made it into a scary story, and some of them won't stay at night because old Ella might get them and she's dead.

All the corn, wheat, and soybeans grown on our farm are grown on land we have leased out, and we leased our land because we couldn't afford to buy the equipment farmers use these days. So with the strawberry selling and the pumpkins in the fall, and the camps, the farm has gotten to be more of a community farm than a regular farm.

CHANGE AND LOSS

Chapter Twenty-Two

Our farm is a great place to live. Sitting on our porch is just wonderful, night or day. Our three sons and all of our grandchildren live on the place, too. But we are only three miles west of Franklin, and the population of Williamson County is exploding. The 1500 acres right across the highway from us is being developed, and the area around us is changing fast, too. During the summer it should be okay, but when the leaves aren't on the trees, we are going to see lots of lights over there at night. There's no telling how many streetlights there are going to be. But my biggest concern is that every drop of rain that falls over on that 1500 acres, every drop of it,

drains through our farm on its way to the West Harpeth River. We depend on the purity of that water, and I am concerned about what might

West Harpeth River

176

happen to our livelihood. If they spray herbicides and insecticides on their golf course, that could run down through our farm to our livestock. We will just have to learn to live with all the increased traffic.

Along with what is coming across the highway, the TVA is deciding where they are going to come across our farm with the new power lines they are running. The first plan they came up with almost cut our land in half, but later on they promised they wouldn't do that. They said, "We're not going to cut your farm in two." I just want it to work out the best way it can.

Everything started changing after World War Two, but I don't think people around here realized it at first. When the war ended, a lot more people started having money, and they wanted to live out in the country. For a long time it wasn't too noticeable, but in the last twenty years the change has been unbelievable.

Franklin has changed a lot. I can walk down Main Street on Saturday and there won't be many people, and I probably won't know any of them. The way it used to be is history. Most people don't have any idea of the way it was. The Main Street that I knew has gone so far away. Sometimes I go over to the Cool Springs Mall, which is the biggest commercial center in Williamson County. I can sit down on a bench, and if I am lucky I might see one person I know out of every six or seven hundred who walk by. I don't know where all the people are coming from.

And the changes that came with the war involved more than just where people lived. We didn't have much before, and then along came that terrible war and we wanted our children to have everything we could give them. The big thing for us when I was young was to go to a picture show, but pretty soon everybody had a television. Most people didn't have automobiles before the war, and then almost everybody had one or two. So a lot of things were lost when so many people came in, and a lot more was lost when we got so much. We lost everybody knowing everybody else. We lost having nothing to be scared of but rabid dogs, and we lost having

177

the worst criminals be chicken thieves and bootleggers. We lost open land and a lot of natural beauty. We lost living in a place where our children were safe—where they could go off and learn some of the lessons of life along creeks and rivers, and out in the woods and the fields.

Our favorite hunting and fishing was up on what we called the Pointer Place, and on a creek near there. Now it is subdivisions all the way to the Interstate. When I went to see my friend, Huddy, there were just fields and woods. Now you'd have to get past 150 or 200 houses to get to his house from where I used to live. That is what hurts me the most—that's the one that really just took it away from me. There won't be hunting or fishing there anymore. That is where we dug our sassafras, where the bees were, and where we did all kinds of things. There was a place where I used to stop and drink from a spring that came out from under some rocks. Nothing was there but woods, but now there are houses all around. I am not sure, but the Mack Hatcher Parkway might have gone through where it was. The places where I lived my childhood are all roads and houses now.

I did so many things that the children who live here now can't do anymore. I don't know how many of them could climb a tree and catch a squirrel. There aren't as many rock fences to chase a rabbit into, but then there aren't nearly as many rabbits either. One of the biggest changes I see is the number of quail and rabbits. It used to be no problem to catch as many rabbits or kill as many quail as you wanted, but now they are few and far between. Their habitat has been turned into subdivisions.

There aren't as many fish as there were when I was a boy. The creeks in Williamson County have changed. We went bare-footed in all the creeks, and we never worried about cutting our feet on glass or cans or other trash. The water was all pretty well clear. Back then the Big Harpeth had a lot of white suckers, which some people called white horses or red horses. I don't ever see them any more. They were not good fish, but the fact that there aren't as many tells me that the water has changed. It is just not as clean and clear as it once was. The West Harpeth is still a pretty good stream, but I don't know about the Big Harpeth. There are still fish in the Big Harpeth, but nothing like we had when I was growing up. There was a time when I drank out of all the rivers and creeks around here, but I wouldn't dare do that now.

I know there are different ways of looking at growth. If you don't furnish people with houses and places to live, they won't come. Then again, it seems like property owners should have the right to sell their property if they want to. But should the people who are already here be forced to pay for all the new schools, and for everything else that comes with a lot of new people? I just hope and pray that we can keep our farm. If we can, twenty or thirty years from now somebody might drive down the road and say, "There's a farm. Isn't it strange looking?"

It seems like every time I look up, I see another development. I know we can't keep the county the way it's been, but we need to get to the place where we can have some restrictions that will at least slow it down. Things are just going too fast. Sometimes I get tired of thinking about it. I want to enjoy my life, and one of the things I love to do is look back on the life I have had. I couldn't have grown up in a better place than Williamson County.

EPILOGUE

I look back at my boyhood and I think about the wonderful place where we lived and the good life we had, even though we didn't have anything—even though we lost my father. I look back on how I came to love athletics, and I can see how much they did for me. I loved playing sports when I was in school. Sports really toughened me up. I learned to knock around for myself, and sports helped me during the worst part of the fighting I experienced. I think sports also helped me be more responsible, and being responsible is probably the most important trait that anybody can have in the military. And then after the war, sports helped provide me with a livelihood for over fifty years.

I look back at the war, and I think about my brother, David. He was killed by Germans, but I don't hate them. Our culture was not the only culture. The German soldiers were somebody's sons and brothers, too. When I look back at the war, I think of Sergeant LaCaze, and I think about God. When Sergeant LaCaze made us learn those ten General Orders, he knew that we needed to know the rules first, then he made sure that we followed them. It is so much like the Ten Commandments. If you know the Ten Commandments and you follow them, you are going to do pretty well in your life.

I came into combat late in the war, but those who came in late and got killed were just as dead as those who died early. I had two or three exceptional experiences, but I look at myself as having been just an average foot soldier. Every soldier who has been in combat has stories to tell. I came through it alive thanks to God, thanks to Sergeant LaCaze, and thanks to the other men in my squad.

When I give a talk about the war, I want the young people in the audience to know that they are in a war, too, but it is a different kind of war. We knew who our enemies were back when we were fighting over in Europe. They had black helmets, bluish-gray uniforms, and they spoke German. Today young people don't recognize their enemies—too much television, the wrong kinds of movies and music, drugs, too many pressures, and having it too easy. We want our children to have everything, and we don't give them enough responsibility in return. I didn't have very much when I was growing up, but what I had was all that I needed.

I look back on all those long, full years after the war, and I think of Mr. Yates and Mr. Thompson and Ernest McCord, and I think about so many of the boys and girls and teachers I knew at Franklin High School. There was Mr. Akin and all the other people who made Battle Ground Academy such a fine school, and Coach Flatt and all the great faculty and kids at Brentwood Academy. Many of the things I have done in my life were with men and boys, but that doesn't make the girls and women I have been close to any less important. In addition to my aunts and sisters-in-law and daughters-in-law, the young ladies I have had in class and the lady associates I've had in schools over the years have made up a wonderful part of my life.

I began by saying, "In the beginning God allowed me to be born into a large family," and I have come to realize that my family includes the thousands of people I have learned from, and taught, over the years. There are hundreds and hundreds of people who have enriched my life. They are part of my story, and I wish I could have mentioned them all in this book, but I decided not to do that.

The list would be like the names in a telephone book—there wouldn't be nearly enough detail, and I knew I would end up leaving too many people out. I hope it is enough to say that God has blessed me with a wonderful extended family that is still growing.

My greatest gift has always been my family. They come out to our house every Christmas. We always have a great big tree, and it's wonderful to have everybody get together. Of the nine children in my family growing up, seven are still living. I have been blessed with children, and I am proud of each and every one of them. And after all is said and  done, there are two people who stand out in my life, Mama—who died in 1980, and my wife of fifty-six years, Rebecca.

When I said "I do" back on August 28, 1946, so help me God I meant it. Rebecca became part of me, and we gave each other three wonderful sons in Jim, Allen, and Scott. We have five grandchildren—Jase, Laura, Mary Morgan, John Fielding, and Hope. Sometimes when I am alone or when I'm driving or walking on the farm, I smile because I'm so proud of them. I thank God for the family He has allowed me to have. And I thank God for the *life* He has allowed me to have.

INDEX

Barker, Roy 133

Battle Ground Academy 51, 71, 72, 142, 148, 150, 154, 155, 157, 158, 170, 174, 181

Battle of the Bulge 99

Baugh, Ella 175

Baugh, George 169, 170, 175

Baugh, Miss Johnnie 139

Bay City, Michigan 89

Bear Wallow 50

Beard, Vernon 50

Bed Check Charlie 91

Bell, Caroline 49

Bell Telephone Company 9, 10, 25

Bethesda 140, 141

Binkley, Louise
    see Louise Gentry

Blue Ribbon Day 49

Bowling Green, Kentucky 37

Boyle, Mississippi 32

Bradley's Bend 153

Brausebad 121

Brentwood Academy 158, 160, 161, 162, 163, 164, 165, 166, 167, 181

Briggs, George 71

Briggs, James 89

Bronze Star 106

Brown, Bill 154, 155

Buchdorf 113, 114, 116

Buford, Fred 64

Burchett, Scobie 132

Butner, George 12

Butner, Gertrude 10
    see also Gertrude Gentry

Butner, John 10

C.P. Daniels' Grocery 62
Cameron, Bill 12
Camp Atterberry 130
Camp Blanding 81, 82
Camp Campbell 8, 133
Camp Kilmer 82, 94, 130
Camp Marcus Orr 128
Camp McPherson 80
Campbell, Brother 156
Campbell, John 27, 39
Cannon, Henry 44, 133, 134
Cannon House 11
Carter House 147
Cartwright, Harold 170
Chadwell, Beverly 86, 132
Channell, Corinne 169, 170
Channell, Rebecca 49, 50, 72, 73, 74, 77, 78, 79, 82, 92, 93, 130,
    131, 133
        see also Rebecca Gentry
Chelsea cigarettes 94
Cherry, Bill 157
Clarksville, Tennessee 130, 131
College Grove 140, 151
Colley, Sarah 45
Collins, General Harry 126
Colonial Bread Company 61
Cook, Lloyd 62
Cookeville, Tennessee 135, 136
Cool Springs Mall 177
County Center 140
Crockett's Store 62
Cullman, Alabama 10
Cumberland Presbyterian Church 14
Cunningham, Boom Boom 135
Czechoslovakia 122

Dachau Concentration Camp 117, 120, 164, 165, 166, 167
Dalton, Ray 150, 159
Danube River 116
Denbo, Don 156
DiMaggio, Joe 33
Doss, Lacy 66
Drill platoon 126
Dugger Ahearn's Store 62

Eagle defense 142
Eanes, Jimmy 152
Ed Thurman's Store 62
English Channel 85
Epworth Church 58
Ewing, Baxter 62, 134
Ewing, Dorthy 37, 131, 134
        see also Dorthy Gentry

Farley, John 89
Farnsworth Lumber Co. 56
Feldkirchen, Austria 7, 127
Fifth Avenue 55, 79, 139, 146, 149, 151
First Presbyterian Church 22, 133
Five Points 14, 22, 62
Fiveash, L. L. 25
Flatt, Carlton 157, 158, 159, 162, 181
Fort Bragg 133
Ford, Harry 156
Fort Oglethorpe 80
Fourth Avenue Church of Christ 35, 68
Frankfurt 129
Franklin Elementary School 22, 36, 49, 50
Franklin High School 9, 34, 59, 69, 120, 136, 139, 146, 148, 149,
        151, 155, 157, 169, 181
Franklin, Marvin 157
Franklin Road 132

Franklin, Tennessee 8, 14, 15, 49, 51, 61, 62, 64, 65, 71, 76, 78,
    83, 93, 118, 129, 132, 133, 136, 138, 139, 140, 150, 176, 177
French Occupation Zone 127
Frost, Ken 145, 146

Garner, Oscar 17, 56, 57
General Linden 96
Genoa, Italy 126
Gentry, Allen 146, 151, 173, 174, 182
Gentry, Bobby 11, 12, 20, 61, 66, 74, 131, 137, 138, 140, 141, 147,
    156, 159
Gentry, Cindy 173, 174
Gentry, Dan 11, 12, 17, 38, 42, 43, 44, 45, 54, 57, 58, 59, 60, 65,
    137, 138, 151, 152, 153
Gentry, David 11, 12, 60, 61, 69, 70, 75, 76, 79, 132, 138, 180
Gentry, Dorthy 10, 23
Gentry, Emma 18
Gentry Farm 169, 173
Gentry, Gertrude 14, 15, 21, 25, 29, 36, 38, 40, 41, 48, 50, 51, 52,
    53, 54, 56, 70, 75, 76, 79, 82, 94, 127, 132, 138, 164, 182
Gentry, Henry 18, 29
Gentry, Hope 182
Gentry, Jase 182
Gentry, Jesse 10
Gentry, Jim 139, 151, 182
Gentry, John Fielding 182
Gentry, Laura 182
Gentry, Louise 10, 82
Gentry, Mary Morgan 182
Gentry, Rebecca 7, 8, 134, 135, 139, 146, 151, 167, 169, 170, 182
Gentry, Scott 149, 151, 158, 170, 182
Gentry, Shotgun 45
        see also Dan Gentry
Gentry, Susie 14
Gentry, William 11, 25, 27, 109, 137, 138
Gentry, Zebulon B. 9, 10, 24, 25, 26, 27, 28, 29, 34, 36, 37, 38, 52,
    151

German, Dr. Dan 45
Giles, George 62
Gizelle, Save the Children 166
Glass, Samuel Fielding 169
Glass, Sara 169
Gracey, Pete 72
Grand Ole Opry 64
Gray, Jessie 48
Gray's Drugstore 61, 69, 70
Guffee, Harry 20, 72, 135
Gunter, Donna 18, 23, 29

H. G. Hill's Store 62
Haffner, Campbell 45
Hale, Missouri 89
Hamilton's Creek 152
Harding, J. A. 25
Hardison, J.A. 83
Harmon, Frances 11, 12, 82, 131
Harmon, Horace 11
Harper, Raymond 62
Harpeth River 16, 24, 36, 47, 55, 56, 116, 153, 179
Harris, Wendell 159
Hart, Carl 89, 91, 92
Haun, A. J. 15, 48, 49
Henderson, Captain Tom 16
Henderson, King 71
Hersh, Gizelle 166, 167
Hillsboro School 51, 140
Hitler, Adolph 128
Holocaust 165
Howard, Dr. 135
Hudler, Maria 168
Hughes, Harvel 55
Hunter, Floyd 143, 144

Inman, Robert 147, 172
Inman, Wayne 147
Interurban bus 140
Irvin, Chick 147

Jacobs, Mickey 159
Jefferson, Alva 83, 133
Jennette's Grocery 62
Jennings, Bob 80
Johnson, Sam 18, 19
Johnston, David 140, 150
Johnston, E. T. 56
Jones, Ethel 48, 50
Jordan, Helen 15

K-rations 94, 100
Kelton, Si 64
King, Billy 136, 143, 162
King, Peter 162
King, Toby 162
King, William 136
Kinnard, C. H. 66, 67
Korean War 163

Lamore, Irving 165
Lavender, Mary 77
Lawson, Riley 13
Le Havre 86, 129
Lee, Tito 163
Lewisburg Avenue 21
Lewisburg Pike 16, 24, 65, 152
Liberty Pike 30
Limb lining 57, 152
Lindberg, Lieutenant John 114